John MacDouall

Narrative of A Voyage to Patagonia and Terra del Fuego

weitsuechtig

John MacDouall

Narrative of A Voyage to Patagonia and Terra del Fuego

ISBN/EAN: 9783943850765

Auflage: 1

Erscheinungsjahr: 2013

Erscheinungsort: Bremen, Deutschland

weitsuechtig

Native of Terra del Fuego.

NARRATIVE OF A VOYAGE

TO

PATAGONIA

AND

TERRA DEL FUEGO,

THROUGH THE STRAITS OF MAGELLAN,

IN H.M.S. ADVENTURE AND BEAGLE, IN 1826 AND 1827.

BY JOHN MACDOUALL, R.N.

"——— Zounds, I'll print it!
Your int'rest Sir.———"

POPE.

LONDON:
RENSHAW AND RUSH, 356, STRAND.

MDCCCXXXIII.

PREFACE.

I DO not find much difficulty in explaining the motives which induced me to offer this Narrative for publication. Whether it will be well or ill-received, I cannot possibly determine. I hope for the best. I have written it not only with the vi w of gain (always pleasant, though sometimes fallacious, as the mirage of the desert to the thirst-parched pilgrim), but also, I am justified in adding, with that of ridding myself of the remarks of certain kind-hearted people, yclept friends, *toujours prêt* at pointing out what ought to be done on all possible occasions. These benevolent personages were continually worrying me in my joyous ruminations with the reiteration of their kind wishes and wonderings, usually rounded off with a " why don't you publish?" followed by the good-natured remarks of "no resolution—want of energy—vague aspirations—*et id genus omne.*" Should I not attempt, I shall be upbraided and vilified, or failing in the attempt I shall be laughed at: a pleasant alternative. The latter, however, in common with my superiors and my more practised brethren in the art of writing, I must be content to endure. Criticism claims it as a right to find or make her victims.

A fine opportunity is now offered for any affluent and high-minded individuals to exercise the influence with which a happier fortune, and it may be more *sterling* deserts, have invested them in favour of one whose visit to *Port Famine,* and some time residence on that inhospitable coast, have left no wish of *re*-visiting it, really or metaphorically—"I lack advancement."

NARRATIVE OF A VOYAGE

TO

PATAGONIA AND TERRA DEL FUÉGO,

IN 1826 AND 1827.

HIS Majesty's surveying vessels, Adventure and Beagle, left Plymouth Sound on the 22d May, 1826, destined to survey a part of the great continent of South America, not only comprising the unfrequented part of Patagonia and Terra del Fuégo, but more particularly to determine the practicability of a passage through the Straits of Magellan: a voyage which had hitherto nearly baffled the skill and calculations of the preceding navigators, Bourgainville, Cordoba, and Wallis, and proved so fatal to a part of the ship's company of H. M. S. Wager, on their voyage homeward through these desolate and cheerless straits. Such had been the extreme hazard in passing the various terrors encountered between the rugged shores of Patagonia and Terra del Fuégo, that most commanders had been intimidated from proceeding homeward through these famous straits; and they had been generally considered as presenting too formidable a prospect for attempting, and looked upon almost as unnavigable.

After a fine voyage of eight days we made the Island of Madeira, a place not requiring much description at the present day; and well known, from the salubrity and genial temperature of its climate, to be much resorted to by the sickly and consumptive. If a Portuguese merchant has occasion to be absent from Madeira for a short period of time, he hurries his loving and weeping wife to an institution, remarkable for its dreary appearance and barred windows, where she is secreted and watched, much against her opinion of the propriety of it, until his return; and, like the maid servant in many good worldly families, is not allowed any followers. She is to be seen as the evening sets in with a pale melancholy face at the grated windows, casting many a wistful look upon the Plaza, and sighing, like Yorick's starling, "I can't get out." If the ladies of this island are accused or suspected of entertaining too great an inclination to gallantry, does not the restraint laid upon them by their husbands in a great measure contribute to it?

> "Danae, though shut within a brazen tower,
> Felt the male virtue of a golden shower;
> But chaste Penelope, left to her own will,
> And free disposal, never thought of ill."

An instance tending to illustrate this position occurred during our stay at Madeira, which shows that they sometimes, on their release, sufficiently revenge themselves for their rigorous punishment, but with such peculiar secresy and cunning as seldom to subject themselves to the unwelcome intrusion of their suspicious husbands; although it generally happens that there is some well-wishing person ready to whisper to the husband the tricks of his pretty wife, otherwise he is generally the last to know it. A lady of some consideration in the island took it into her head to make an Irish gentleman, a resident there likewise, the object of her better choice; now, as it is one of the whims of a Portuguese lady to possess, at any risk, what she admires, provided she is not slighted, she soon contrived to convince this person of her partiality, and he, being a gallant man, treated her with a becoming politeness. The lady suddenly grew very religious, and was so fond of going to mass and to implore the protection of "Nossa Senhora," that the husband—good, unsuspicious man—secretly congratulated himself on possessing a lady so sensible and good, and who made him the happiest man in the world. It was one of those *whisperings* before alluded to that startled him, and made him ask the lady, on her return, the reason of her quitting home so very often. "I go," said she, with much humility in her look, "to kneel before Nossa Senhora." However, the next time she went out, he followed the palanquin and the steps of his tripping wife, not to the cathedral, but to a house in the suburbs of the town—he gained admittance, approached the room *à tâtons*, and found that the *religieuse*, instead of performing a genuflexion before "Nossa Senhora," was encircling the brawny neck of a broad-shouldered Irishman, who seemed perfectly content in his temporary imprisonment in the delicate arms of this Portuguese lady. Contrary to the custom of a Portuguese, he did not stab the Hibernian, but he sent his wife off the island. No doubt the *dénouement* did not turn out so agreeable as she anticipated, but the place of her exile and penance was never discovered. The people of this island are certainly fond of music and revelry, for even at midnight the sound of the guitar and piano salutes the ear from the houses in every quarter. They have no lunatic asylum, although many persons have the appearance of being dangerously insane; and as for the halt and the lame, I never beheld such a grievous heap of leprous beggars, dragging their bodies after them, with their paralysed legs and arms dangling in the most artless manner by their sides. Some, indeed, there are, notwithstanding their being doomed to crutches, who amble along very stoutly, reminding you of the answer of Le Diable Boiteux, Asmodeus, to Don

Cleophas: "*Tout estropié que je suis je ne laisse pas d'aller bon train.*" The prisoners in the gaol or receptacle for felons and murderers (and it is generally well filled) have no resource while incarcerated to keep themselves from starving, as there is no gaol allowance, but a precarious dependance upon eleemosynary aid; and you may see many uncouth and malignant visages protruding through the gratings of the prison, holding in their hands a string, to which is attached a small bag to receive donations from the charitably disposed. In this manner the smallest coin is quickly drawn up, and instantly descends with the deafening outcry of "*Misericordia hum pobre Portuguez*:" occasionally a regular scramble takes place among them when one receives a larger contribution than another.

The monasteries are grey and venerable edifices; but were I to mention the disgraceful and infamous conduct pursued by the priests and monks on this island, a person could not but feel exasperated at these "greasy rogues," who in reality commit more sin than all the rest of the inhabitants put together. Much might be said in praise of the surrounding country and scenery, which is delightful, but Madeira has been so fully and frequently described, that it would be superfluous in me to detain the reader with any further comment, now we are about to bid adieu, in feeble imitation of Byron's Adieu to Malta, (the Hibernian must pardon me) to this gem of the ocean.

Adieu, Madeira, sunny island,
Alas! I can no longer spy land:
Adieu, the narrow dirty town;
Adieu, to monk and shaven crown;
Adieu, *chaste* Nun, whose thoughts are given
To find the nearest way to heaven;
Adieu, those monasteries grey,
Where innocence is led astray;
Adieu, the Friar's salacious chuckle—
How surely ye do swill and guttle;
Adieu, the bower and orange grove,
In which intriguing lovers rove;
Adieu, each saintly glittering thing,
Pride, vermin, fish, and palanquin;
Adieu to gloom and convents dreary,
Rosary, cross, and Virgin Mary,
To "Clementina,*" placid, pale,
A victim to the sacred veil;

* Clementina, the youngest, and one of the most amiable of a Portuguese family, was, by the decree of her parents, forced to take the veil. She appears to be so reconciled and devoted to her fate, that a removal now from the seclusion of the monastery would

Adieu, cool mountains, valleys, *foute*,
And "Nossa Senhora da Monte*;"
Adieu, those vineyards, which so cool are,
Leprous beggars, wilful "Mula†,"
Confession-box so neatly built,
Stern Abbess, yielding nuns, and guilt.
Adieu, those stories nuns can tell,
By friars shrived in lonely cell;
They think the task that he imposes
A tumble on a bed of roses;
To see the kisses they can number,
And merely check them when they slumber,
Amusement for their lips and fingers,
A small rebuke when virtue lingers;
O, blousy friar! O, padres mine!
Perhaps my best wish you 'll decline—
It is to have ye on the line—
Not that of hemp—but Neptune's brine,
There for a time to change our station,
That we might grant *you* dispensation,

---

be even more painful to her mind than the feeling she experienced at her entrance on her noviciate.

* "Our Lady of the Mountain." A church so called, and situated on a mountain about three miles from the town. This church is plainly to be perceived long before you enter the Bay of Funchal.

† "Mula." All persons who have been at Madeira must recollect this cry. The swarthy muleteers have a long pole with which they beat and drive on these obstinate animals, and at every bang they loudly cry out "mula," and unless these sounds are repeated every ten paces, the mules will not move at all—unless the stick accompaniment compels them.

For much I'd rather you than we
Should duck'd, and tarr'd, and feather'd be;
But, "I must onward, doom'd to sail,"
Whence these unhappy things prevail,
So fare thee well, sweet isle prolific
In sins, to suit these *strains pacific.*

In a few days we weighed anchor, and shaped our course for Teneriffe, which we made after a very short run, and came too in Santa Cruz roads on the morning of the 8th June. This island is likewise well known, so famous for its majestic peak. There is a good cathedral, and the town from the harbour is pretty enough. Sunday (as is the custom in most countries where the Roman Catholic religion prevails) is set aside for displaying the "Mantillas," and the pretty feet of the young Donzellas. The Spanish women are unquestionably very superior to the Portuguese, both in general *naïvetè* of manner and elegance of person, and their dispositions are more liberal and free than those of the females of Madeira. Perhaps the idea of elegantly dressed ladies chatting familiarly on the Plaza with the low Spanish soldiery may be thought incompatible with the Spanish pride, yet custom here does not forbid it, and it is of frequent occurrence. The soldiers, by the by, have great good manners, and show themselves worthy of the compliment. These Spanish ladies, I believe, cannot boast of their mental acquirements, for as long as they can revel in all the splendour of dress and equipage, and give you a volley from a pair of black eyes that would warm the heart of an anchorite, they are regardless about them, paying much more attention to the study of the fan *, and its expressive movements, than devotion to the chaste instructions of the aya or governess, or the gentle and soothing whispers of their pious padré.

The general habit and character of the Spaniards is manifested even on this small island in that inseparable hauteur so habitual to them, and their actions partake of the gross superstition so common among the inhabitants of Old Spain, and some instances of which may be considered as absurd enough, such as crossing

* It is well known that the Spanish ladies have a perfect language with the fan, and can convey, by their manner of using it, their sentiments either of esteem or dislike.

themselves when they chance to gape to prevent the Devil going down their throats, or, should they happen to sneeze, the "muchas gracias," (many thanks) given to a stranger for crying out "Jesus," for the same reason; and herein they seem to act in accord with our old custom of responding "God bless you" to such sternutatory salutes. A national indolence and disinclination to any exertion during mid-day, a bibbing of coffee, and the *siesta*, form their luxuries, while some, with sedate and Quixotic countenances, practise the Turkish system, in the enjoyment of their own ideas and a cigar—indeed, without one of the latter, a Spaniard appears to be lost. They seem happy and content as long as they can blow a slow, steady stream of smoke, which gives way only for the theatre, the ball, the serenade, and the intrigue; and I believe they do not pretend to a superior degree of purity in that respect. The hotels are large and well conducted, and the rooms are on a very extended scale and furnished with a peculiar neatness; but, although the living here is good and cheap, it takes some time before you can relish their garlic and grease. You meet with a good deal of civility, induced, no doubt, by the expectation of the ready-money system; and here, indeed, they seem to understand, perfectly well, the character of the English sailor, who never appears satisfied unless he is allowed to make more noise than any other person, and is charged double the price that would be asked from an individual of any other nation. After a short stay here, we bore away for the Cape de Verd Islands, experiencing nothing on the voyage but fair weather and sunny skies. On our arrival at St. Antonio the heat was so suffocating and oppressive (while lying-to under the lee of the island) that all on board were gasping for breath and becoming plaguy ill-tempered. Our ship now began, as it were, to stink most confoundedly, and the captain and officers on board were very busy in endeavouring to find out the cause. In vain was brimstone burnt and gunpowder exploded, the stench continued, " a very ancient and fish-like smell." Every one on board thought at first that it proceeded from the gun-room, the officers being of the same opinion themselves, and accordingly all the store-rooms were rummaged for the damaged provisions, and the gun-room steward was indefatigable in searching, unpacking, and re-stowing their stock; but although there was a *rank* compound of *villanous* smells in their store-room, yet nothing was found bad enough to occasion the stench which affected the whole ship's company. While thus engaged, the poor steward was so unlucky as to throw down and break some bottles of ale belonging to the purser, a man fond of "ortolans and green peas," in short, an epicurean, by whom he was not likely to be forgiven. At last one of the lieutenants, an excellent-hearted, jocose, good-humoured fellow came to the "Middy's berth," determined in his own mind to overhaul all the lockers. In vain we protested it could not exist with us; he proceeded to rouse out everything, and at one of the cupboards, as he continued the search, we observed his nostrils dilate amazingly, and on turning round to look at us, observing we were all upon the broad grin, he thrust his arm down and brought up a keg of pickled fish (purchased at Plymouth); which the hot weather had rendered putrescent; this, with a cask of Irish butter, had occasioned the nuisance. As there was a great necessity for having them thrown overboard, it was done immediately, not without regret on our part; for when we came to consider the tedious voyage across the Atlantic, as this was the chief part of our private stock, it took us some time to be reconciled to the event. However, we affected much mirth, jollity, and unconcern, and, with the ordinary comforts of gin, and biscuits and cheese, proceeded merrily enough, notwithstanding the cookery of our steward, "a wretched ragged man," who seemed to have a great attachment to dirt.

To give the *coup de grace* to our situation, the clerk, "he seeks no better name," being wanted upon deck, was suddenly aroused from sleep, (for all in our berth liked to sleep after dinner), and jumping from the locker upon which he was reclining, stood up in a barrel containing about 150 eggs, and smashed the greater part of them; this was owing, in some degree, to our careless steward, who had placed the cask, without the lid upon it, right under the feet of the somniferous scribe. And, oh! all ye who suffer from sea-sickness, whether you are of a tough and sinewy nature, or are unfortunately of a delicate constitution, let me, from experience, caution you, when afflicted by the said visitation, not to pour "hot and rebellious liquors in your blood," but solace yourself with making a meal from that kind of scum which the cook skimmed up for Sancho Panza, when that worthy squire "begged that he might be permitted to sop a luncheon of bread in one of the jar-pots" of Camacho the rich: such fare, with a draught of smart bottled beer, will ultimately prove more beneficial than with any kind of wine, from renowned Burgundy to "imperial Tokay."

St. Jago was the next island we touched at; it is subject to the Portuguese, and a rare sky-rocketing set they are. The town is situate on an elevated point of land, and has a very mediocre appearance. The surrounding scenery is bold and striking. I shall spare myself the trouble of detailing the monotonous course of a long sea voyage, and a recapitulation of the trifling incidents which occur to relieve the wear and tear of the mind, and of that kind of feeling which, in despite of all mastery, will sneak into your behaviour from being constantly in company with the same persons, who, perhaps, possess a total dissimilarity of disposition, and some of whom are not much skilled in the "*savoir vivre,*"—who would not prefer a Trinculo to a Caliban?

We arrived at Rio de Janeiro on the 9th of August; on nearing the entrance of this harbour, a stranger cannot but admire the bold outline and general appearance of the surrounding scenery. On the left of the approach to the interior is a conical mountain, rising from the sea to the height of nine hundred feet, called the Sugar loaf *(pan de Azuca);* it is a species of granite, and has on the top a few stumps of stunted brush-wood. This mountain differs from all others on the coast, as it inclines to the westward, and the rest to the eastward. On the opposite side of the entrance is the fortress of Santa Cruz, situated on a bold projecting point of land, entirely commanding the entrance of the harbour; it has three tiers of guns, amounting in all to ninety-six, of various calibres; it is at present in a good state of defence; there is a small fixed light-house upon it. In the middle of the mouth of the harbour there is an octagon fort, called Lagé, mounting about thirty guns; and further on is Fort Vilganhon, situated on a small island of that name, and mounting about thirty-six guns: this fort is three miles from that at Santa Cruz. There are two other forts on the right hand side, about two miles from the entrance, but they are not garrisoned, being entirely out of repair. After passing this fort, you gain a highly picturesque view of the town of San Sebastian, formed between two hills. On the top of each a monastery is situated; one formerly belonged to the Jesuits, but is now an hospital, the other to the Benedictines, at present a guard house. The appearance of the numerous cupolas and steeples, overtopping the houses, forms a striking contrast to the mountainous country in perspective. Nearly opposite to the town is the island of Cobrás, so designated from the quantities of snakes found on it when the first settlement was made there. On this island the state prison is built, and the formidable battery by which it is defended not only commands the greater proportion of the harbour, but likewise the town and dock-yard. The fort, however, is at present but indifferently guarded. When a vessel arrives here, she is boarded by the health-boat, before any person is permitted to land. Immediately on landing at the palace stairs, the eye is attracted to a large white building, called the emperor's palace; it is certainly strongly built, and exceedingly plain; and under the porticos are to be seen, skulking, at all hours, the mulatto soldiers attached to the Brazilian service. On the right of the landing-place is the fountain, a neat stone building, surmounted by the Portuguesé arms. This conduit is supplied with water from various springs, which concentrate, and form in the hollow of a mountain, called the "Corcovado," (Hunchback,) the height of which above the level of the sea is 2,300 feet, and it forms the highest point of land, excepting the Tejuca, seen from the harbour. The streets in the town are dirty and narrow; and at the corner of most of the principal is to be seen the figure of the Virgin Mary (precious image), or other saint; and, to prevent the influence of a vertical sun upon her sweet countenance, they are considerate enough to encircle her during the day with painted curtains, where she remains "*perdue*," until evening, when she is most splendidly surrounded with lamps. The Virgin is made to smile most benignantly upon the bowing hypocritical Portuguese, a benefit which the base and shaven-crowned friars most piously enjoy while prostrating themselves before her. These people have little to do; they solicit alms the whole day, and at evening assemble to carouse and revel on the spoil obtained by begging and imposition. "*Por la noche nos Juntábamos, y nos réiamos de los que se habian compadécido de nosotros por el dia.*"—GIL BLAS.

The principal squares are the Campo de St. Anna, the Constitution, and that of the Palace.

The Campo, much the largest of the three, is in length about four hundred yards, and in breadth three hundred. In this square is the hospital for vaccination, which is open every feast day to any person wishing to be vaccinated gratuitously—all slaves on their arrival are vaccinated. You can perceive from this square, a few hundred yards to the right, on the hill above the aqueduct, the venerable nunnery of Santa Térésa, a white edifice, with one spire. The difficulty of access to the interior alone precludes the possibility of giving a minute detail; but, speaking from general report, the nuns who exist there at this time have long passed their climacteric. The emperor, it is said, has an eye to the property attached to the nunnery, for, on the demise of the nuns, by his peremptory order *no noviciates being allowed to enter,* it necessarily falls to the crown. The square called the Constitution is a bout three hundred yards in length, and two hundred in breadth; in the middle is erected a pillar, twenty feet in height, on the top of which is a brass globe, although I cannot say it adds much to the beauty of the square; the houses on either side are regular and well-built, but partaking of the usual formation as to lowness of construction. The Opera House is situated in this square, and is a tolerably handsome structure. The interior is lightly and rather tastefully decorated, and has four tiers of boxes, and each tier is divided into thirteen partitions, or boxes; and you frequently perceive some very gloomy and ochre countenances in the interior. The emperor's box entirely takes up the centre, and is concealed from view by a plain blue fringed curtain, except on particular days or gala nights. The emperor and his suite seldom occupy it; and when he is present, all the audience rise and face him, and only resume their seats when the performance continues. The three first rows in the pit are partitioned off from the remaining seats; and, for the privilege of being nearer to the harsh and inharmonious music in the orchestra (and the musicians are mostly mulattos), you are charged one-third more—the price of admission to the other places in the pit being about half a dollar. The ballet is exceedingly well conducted; the *artistes* are of good talent, and most of them principal dancers from the Parisian theatre. Be it observed, they do not always get paid their salaries, which they say is very disheartening, after coming so far to earn them. The singers are generally the refuse of the Italian Opera on the continent. The opera was usually the rendezvous for most of the gentlemen belonging to his majesty's ships in harbour, to observe the fanciful evolutions of a Mademoiselle Louise, who, although assuredly not the best *danseuse* engaged, had contrived, by a recourse to short petticoats, and the execution of rapid *pirouettes*, to win the admiration and applause of the naval officers, who always seemed to consider, that the higher she jumped, the better she danced; indeed, whenever she appeared, the loud cries of "*Viva Louise*" were heard equally to proceed from steady *luffs* and noisy youngsters. Nor was the gentle Louise at all insensible to this mark of preference, for she always smiled most graciously, and curtsied most gracefully her thanks for the homage paid to her talents. But, alas! Louise got married and lost her slim shape; and one day, while talking to English Mary, in the *rua d'Ouvidor* (and what young officer has not stopped on his cruize to win a smile from kind-hearted English Mary?) she suddenly burst into tears, and said how foolish she had been to get married, for she knew very well that she never would be able to dance again, or gain any more *Vivas* from the English officers. She was however mistaken, for, some months afterwards, I left her pursuing the *tee-totum* system with as much *éclat* as ever.

There is one circumstance which particularly strikes an Englishman,—but whether it proceeds from ancient custom or the habitual jealousy of the Brazilians, I cannot pretend to say,—that no females are permitted to enter the pit.

There is an institution in this city perhaps worth remarking for its singularity: any person desirous of providing for the consequences of his amours, proceeds to the Foundling Hospital, and places the infant in a perpendicular box, which moves on a pivot in the wall, and ringing a bell which is placed there for that purpose, the box is turned, and the child disappears for ever. If it should be a male, it is left to the foundling's option, when grown up, whether he would prefer the army or navy, or like to move in the more humble sphere of an artizan; and if he should make choice of the latter, he is apprenticed to the trade he prefers, and is afterwards set up in it. On a female's attaining the age of thirteen or fourteen, there are certain days in the year when any young man, desirous of matrimony, can enter this place and make choice of any of that sex whom he considers likely to promote his happiness; nevertheless, if the lady does not evince a reciprocity of feeling, she is at liberty to decline his advances; but if she expresses no disinclination, they are married. However, previous to the ceremony taking place, it is required that the person should convince the superiors of the institution that his pursuits in life are adequate to the maintenance of a wife and family; a good sum is then given as a marriage portion. This institution is maintained partly by the emperor, and the inhabitants of Rio support it by voluntary contributions.

Not far from one of their gaols is the slave-market. The slaves of both sexes are exhibited in large rooms hired for that purpose. I went to see them, and my heart was touched with wonder and with pity: they are seated like the audience in the pit of a theatre; the higher benches are occupied by the elder and maturer Africans of the ages of thirty and forty, the middle seats by others from fifteen to twenty, while the lowest are thronged by infants of the tender ages of four and five; and the slavers seem to give the preference to children of such early years, as they are by far the most numerous. Those from fifteen to twenty apparently are utterly regardless of the motives for which they are brought there, but regard you with a vacuity of countenance almost approaching to idiotcy; the elder seem more acutely to feel the horrors of their situation, and recognize in you immediately the slightest expression of kindness: as long as you remain in the room their eye never ceases to follow you—it fixes upon you its gloomy and inquiring gaze, but on the least contraction of your brow, or an indication of anger in your face, it is immediately withdrawn, and they seem to shrink from further observation, so feelingly are they alive to the least trait of unkindness, and so well can they distinguish between gentleness and ferocity. A great many, however, both male and female, of the middle age, appear to evince a happy indifference as to their future fate—they wear a gayer aspect, and to them the horrors of slavery are as nothing; at any rate it did not affect their appetite, for I beheld in one room nearly a hundred in high good humour, and all very busy round different bowls, containing bananas and farina, which they conveyed down their throats (their hands serving for spoons) with great composure and tranquillity, chatting to each other with such a peculiarity of wild gesture and tone, that I determined to ask the ill-conditioned Brazilian, who appeared to have the care of them, what they were talking about. On my putting the question to him in Portuguese, he fixed his small sunken eyes upon me, and said, "*Nao entiende*," giving it the full nasal sound: at the same time he hurried away, as if fearful of any more questions. He now spoke in a loud voice to the dingy throng, and in a moment they were as silent as the grave, not a whisper was heard among them, while the slaver seated himself on a small bench, and eyed me with such scrutiny, and with such "a lurking devil in his sneer," as convinced me he would have had much pleasure in selling me at half price. There were upwards of fifty rooms filled with these poor wretches, and, on a moderate calculation, I did not see less than two thousand. I was one of the merely curious, and had set out determined not to be intimidated by the manners of these slave merchants. It was there I saw, for the first time in my life, this traffic in human flesh carried on with something worse than the sordid feelings that prevail at a horse fair. When a bargain is struck, in many instances their hands are tied, and away they are led. From 150 to 200 dollars is the usual price, but varies according to age and physical ability. When young, they readily acquire the Portuguese language; but those who have reached the maturity of life, never thoroughly learn it. If they are fortunate enough to be purchased by masters who treat them kindly, they cheerfully and faithfully finish the allotted task, and have a look of tranquillity which bespeaks contentment. The following occurrence, however, would show, that sometimes they are capable of committing the deepest villainy. A Portuguese had a settlement in a distant and retired part of the country, and, indeed, was the only inhabitant and master of a place altogether remote from any other estate: he had reared from infancy a slave, named José, and had always treated him with a generosity and kindness that seemed at variance with the generally debased nature and custom of a Portuguese. It happened one day that the master had occasion to chastise José for some neglect of duty, and from that instant the African sought the readiest and most diabolical method of satiating his dark revenge; nor did he wait long for an opportunity. His master was one afternoon repairing a boat, and while in the act of stooping to take up a hammer, José clove his skull with an axe, and dashed his brains, mingled with his grey hairs, upon the ground, hacking the body almost to pieces; he killed the mule upon which his master used to ride, set fire to the house, and fled to the fastnesses in the mountains, there to join the other runaway negroes, who, from the ill treatment of their masters, or their own perverse dispositions, are continually resorting thither.

Slaves committing murder at Rio (for no one is ever hanged there for that crime) are distinguished by parties of them being chained together by the neck and legs, and are employed in carrying water, in wooden buckets, to different parts of the town, the whole day, and in all other severe and laborious drudgery. Whilst thus employed, they are in custody of two of the Brazilian soldiers, armed with bayonets; and as these criminals are allowed to beg, you are frequently accosted by them in the streets. Most of the poorest classes (living in straggling villages within ten miles of the city) have no better habitations than small thatched huts, plastered together with clay, and built of sticks and poles:

and of an evening are often seen women, of a tawny and squalid aspect, squatting outside the doors, either combing their own heads or searching for vermin in the heads of their children (but there is no occasion to go so far out of town to see this, for in Rio such a sight is common enough), and if you talk to them, they still continue their employment, and destroy them, very unceremoniously, before you. Not unfrequently, in the interior of the country, you find a Brazilian settler paired off with a strapping negress, and a family of naked mulatto children frisking before the house:

"Turtles and doves, of different hues, unite,
And glossy jet is paired with shining white."
Pope's Sappho and Phaon.

The ship "Real Principe," which conveyed the royal family from Portugal in 1828 to the Brazils, was converted into a prison-ship, and contained as abandoned and degenerate a race as could be found in any country in the known world. On ascending the side of the ship to the lower deck, it presented a sight which baffles all description. Here were to be seen, in promiscuous and filthy disorder, the male and female convict dragging on a life of supreme wretchedness; some employed in mending their torn and ragged apparel, others in washing and cleaning themselves, in cooking their dinner, or combing their head. The haggard and squalid mechanic burnishes a gun or a sword, the profit of which is to procure him his wretched mess; whilst others, at their respective trades, silently and slowly pursue their respective work. Many, wrapped in the noisome rug, endeavour to sleep away their hunger, others, rendered desperate by reproach or disease, quarrel with their fellow captives, and are only silenced by the appearance of the heavy chains or the sword at their throat, most of them being doomed to linger out their lives in this rank and loathsome place. On the upper deck are confined those convicted of lighter crimes, but it presents the same wretched scene, at which human nature shudders. The busy hum and low murmuring sound of those employed in the most menial offices, or in watching and cooking their scanty fare; the gloominess and stench of the place, and the poor, emaciated, hollow-eyed creatures that are seen crowded together on all sides, suffering from leprosy and other diseases, unpitied and unheeded by the armed sentry, cannot fail to excite an Englishman's pity and commiseration, and make him acknowledge the superiority of his own mild and paternal government over that of all other nations. The daily pittance allowed in the prison-ship is too scanty to support nature, and were it not for the wives of some of the felons (who are allowed free ingress to their husbands), their time would pass most wretchedly. The starved appearance of these women, and their yellow, lean visages, forcibly tell the extreme privation they undergo. It was in the cabin of this ship that I saw the assistant-master of H. M. S. Redwing, suffering a vexatious imprisonment in 1826. I forget the circumstances which led to his capture, but I believe he had been taken at sea (by a Brazilian frigate), on board some brig or schooner (of which he had been put in command), and not having any papers with him, was brought into Rio, and kept on board this ship until inquiry could be made into it. I understood this young man died on his passage to England some months afterwards.

The following adventure, which occurred to a gay and gallant friend of mine, perhaps requires some apology to the reader, but I cannot resist the inclination I feel to insert it, from its comicality. One night, about 12 o'clock (and the streets, at this hour, are deserted and lonely), he met a party of Brazilian ladies and gentlemen, who were apparently returning from some place of amusement; but there was a young lady forming one of the company who very soon attracted his attention, and she was walking a little behind them, followed by a little black girl (her servant.) As he passed close to her, he saw, or thought he saw, her smile; but being in some doubt about it, he turned his head round, and was looking after her, when the little girl came by him, and it was impossible not to perceive the large white teeth of this dingy attendant, who smiled, or rather laughed, in a very agreeable manner; and as he continued to look after them, he observed that they both turned their heads to look back on him, and he therefore rather quickened his pace, and was induced to follow, which he did silently and cautiously, not wishing to be observed by the persons who were in company. After walking some time, the whole party stopped at a house in the Rua ——, and one of the gentlemen took the lady who had captivated my friend under his care, and they proceeded to a more distant part of the town. He followed close for fear of losing them (as the streets are miserably dark), and the little black slave kept frequently turning her head, to observe whether he was following. They at length stopped at a genteel house, where the gentleman bade her good night, and set off at a quick pace; he noted the house, and went on board. The next day he came on shore and passed the place, and he saw the little negress at the window, who, on recognizing him, instantly withdrew, and in a few minutes the young senhora herself appeared and seated herself by the parlour window. He sauntered leisurely by, and said in Portuguese, as he passed, that "he should come again at 10 o'clock that night," and then walked quickly away, fearful of being observed talking to her. At the hour mentioned, he went accordingly; the house was closed, but he could hear within the sound of the guitar and revelry. He loitered about until 11 o'clock, when three gentlemen, wrapped in large cloaks, left the house. In about half an hour he saw the door open just wide enough to permit the black woolly head of the young slave to peep out, and when she perceived him, she withdrew her head, and left the door upon the jar, and he immediately went forward and stole in unperceived. Without speaking a word, she shut the door, which she fastened instantly, and he was left in complete darkness. He caught hold of her, however, upon which she said, *Espera un poco* (wait a little), and he was left by himself to ruminate on the chances of his being kicked out for his impudence. His sooty conductress soon returned with a candle, and beckoned him to follow, which he did, but not without some fear of being laid hold of by two or three stout negroes, ready to give him some severe admonition; however, his fear soon vanished when he was shown into a room, where, seated on a sofa, he beheld his fair enslaver, who appeared to be as young and beautiful as his imagination had painted. The table was spread with a profusion of fruits and sweetmeats, and a magnum of *vinho porto* stood on a small sideboard at the other side of the room. As he had a tolerable knowledge of the Portuguese language, he was enabled to compliment his fair entertainer, and to express his happiness in being so fortunately introduced to her acquaintance. The little slave, after rolling her dark eyes about, and giving him one of her facetious grins, left them together, and laid herself down upon a mat just outside the door, and soon fell asleep. As near as he could recollect, it was about half-past two in the morning, when he was awoke by a loud knocking and kicking at the door, when the lady started off the couch, exclaiming, *O, cruz, O, cruz! meu marido, meu marido!* and by the light of a small lamp which was dimly burning in one corner, she quickly snatched up his clothes and darted out of the room, beseeching him to follow, which he did in so clumsy a manner, that he trod upon and stumbled over the naked legs and feet of the sleeping black wench, and measured his length upon the floor. The poor black girl, finding herself so rudely assaulted, began crying out also, *Cruz, cruz!* in a very piteous tone of voice. His nimble conductress quickly opened some kind of recess, and throwing in his clothes, pushed him in after them, and shut the door, locked it, and withdrew the key. Being thus shut up in this dark cupboard, he was soon assailed by some very unpleasant reflections, and he could have wished himself in his hammock; but what were his sensations when he found some kind of reptile crawling up his legs, and two or three large winged insects settled at the same time on his face and neck, and running all over him; but he was still more startled to hear a most outrageous quarrel between the lady and a hoarse-voiced gentleman, and he felt much anxiety and trepidation for her fate as well as for his own; yet he was pleased to find that she maintained her ground with a determined spirit in their battle of words; but he presently heard him several times pronounce the word *mato* (kill), and his apprehensions increased again at these fearful sounds, and being locked up and unarmed, he expected the door to be burst open, and a long knife thrust into his vitals. He had, however, determined to defend himself and his fair mistress manfully, although he could find no weapon at hand; but he needed no other than the senhora's tongue, and he concluded her wit had furnished her with the best defence, for, after having been kept in this suspense for more than two hours (during which time they did not cease to quarrel), he heard the outer door slam violently, and in a minute afterwards the young senhora unlocked the door, and waving her finger to and fro, said, *No fáce mal.* She was exceedingly pale, and her long dark hair was unloosed and hung over her face; but she would not allow him to waste time in unavailing caresses or sorrow, but told him to dress and *ora vamos, por amor de dèos* (depart quickly, for God's sake), an intimation he thought too prudent to be neglected. She hastily told him, that on his entrance the first object he cast his eyes upon was his large straw hat, which in her hurry she had forgotten to put out of sight, and he then went off like a rocket.

An Italian gentleman, who was in company when this was related (and he had had some experience in such matters), said a gallant ought never to suffer the door to be opened, as it was always the safest and best to keep an adversary outside the house. I therefore recommend this practice to all who may be placed in a similar predicament. He did not lose sight of this young person, for he had afterwards many opportunities of renewing his acquaintance, which he continued until he left the Brazils for England.

Our armourer on board was, perhaps, one of the ugliest-featured men imaginable, and he would often amuse his shipmates by some singular distortions of visage, which would, perhaps, have rivalled a Turkish grimacer, or even, at humble distance, approach Grimaldi's. It chanced that one of the marines, somehow or other, had got confoundedly drunk—indeed, he was in a state of frenzy from the effect of liquor—

and in this condition he was lying on his back upon the lower deck, just under the armourer (who was then upon the sick-list, and in his hammock), and, possibly, being annoyed by the boisterous noise of the marine, lolled his head over the sides of his hammock, and looked down upon the prostrate "Joe," who kept uttering incoherent sentences about seeing the Devil, when the armourer commenced making the most frightful faces at him, saying, "Here's the Devil." The poor marine had no sooner fixed his staring eyes upon the distorted features of the armourer, than he went into a strong fit, crying out, "I see the Devil; I see him, I see him!" and it was with great difficulty that he was got upon the forecastle, as he raved and struggled in a violent manner, from the fear occasioned by the ugly phiz of the old armourer.

After remaining in the harbour nearly two months, we departed from this chaste city, and encountered, a few days afterwards, a *pampero*, which is a tremendous gale of wind, accompanied with thunder and lightning, that is particularly terrific and vivid. We sometimes fell in with some swinging Buenos Ayrean privateers, who were constantly cruizing in these seas in the hope of picking up some of the Brazilian craft. After a boisterous passage of thirteen days, we anchored in the harbour of Maldonado, Rio de la Plata, and found lying here H.M.S. Ranger, which ship sailed the next day for Monte Video. The Spaniards at this place were rejoiced to see two English ships come in, and the next morning we could perceive a number of people with horses upon the beach, for the conveyance of any person to the town who chose to come on shore. As soon as an opportunity occurred, we visited the town of San Francisco, which is wretchedly built, and situated about two miles inland. We were well received by Donna Francisca de Revaro, who keeps a small *fonda* or hotel (the only one in the place); she is about fifty years of age, and complexioned "like the copper pot in the kitchen," but, in her own opinion, she still possesses charms, for she was fancifully attired, and her head was decorated with a profusion of roses, and she handled a large *ábanico* (fan) with even more grace than her daughter, who soon made her appearance, "at once a slattern and a coquette." She was about four feet high, and fat withal, and possessed that interesting kind of walk that we see displayed by our English milk-women when they shuffle along with the yoke and pails. Donna seemed to be aware of the taste *de los Ingleses,* for she produced for dinner an unmeasurable beefsteak, the only thing, indeed, worthy of commendation, for hard boiled eggs and skinny fowls formed the rest of the eatables: the wine is execrable (Catalan.)

There is some good shooting to be had here, there being plenty of deer about eight or ten miles from the town, and the partridges are of a very large size. You also meet with ducks and teal, the horned and whistling plover, doves, cranes, and numerous other birds.

On the 1st of November, a Brazilian frigate, and some brigs and schooners, stood into the harbour, and anchored close in shore; and as, at this time, a war of extermination existed between the Brazilians and Buenos Ayreans, we expected some disturbance, as the Maldonadians (when the Brazilian ships appeared) hoisted the

Spanish flag; and as there were quartered in the vicinity of Maldonado upwards of two hundred "Gauchos," a determined, and, to the Brazilians, a dreaded foe, we thought that if the Brazilians attempted a landing, they would meet a formidable opposition. The frigate soon commenced firing upon the town, more out of brâvado than in the idea of a shot reaching it, for, as I before observed, it is some distance from the anchorage, and this system of warfare was kept up during the greater part of that and the following day. The Maldonadians were not idle, for they soon mounted on the beach an old twenty-four pounder (the only gun they had); but they were at a loss for ammunition, particularly shot, as they always returned those fired from the frigate. About four hundred yards from the beach we could perceive a considerable force of Gauchos, crouching down behind the different hillocks and banks, to shelter themselves from the showers of grape and cannister poured in upon them by the schooners and brigs. To give some idea of the cowardly behaviour of these Brazilians, a boat pulled off from the frigate, well manned, and rowed towards East Point, in order to land and fetch off some cattle which had strayed there. This intention being perceived on shore, only two Gauchos rode along the beach, and quietly awaited the arrival of the boat's crew, who, not caring to approach too near, rested on their oars when they had arrived at two hundred paces from the shore, and commenced firing at the horsemen, who, nothing daunted, rode down to the water's edge, and returned their shots, and afterwards flourished their swords over their heads, defying them to land. This was quite enough, the boat pulled back again, and the Gauchos returned to their quarters.

There had been left upon the Island of Goritti two sheep, belonging to the gentlemen of the Ranger man-of-war, and a party of these Brazilians had landed on the island, and had worried these poor animals a good deal, until they were made to desist by a party of our men, who were employed on shore; and the next day a letter was sent to Captain King, from the captain of the frigate, putting an interdict upon all further communication with the main-land, thereby cutting off our supplies of "beef and vegetables." This letter called forth a replication from Captain King, in which (I heard) was stated, that every facility was given to ships on a voyage of discovery, even in time of war, by all nations, and also remarking that it would be more to their credit to go and spike the gun on shore than to make war upon a few poor harmless sheep. We heard no more after this about not being suffered to land, and we continued our rambles on shore in spite of this bombardment, which lasted four days, until the frigate and her convoy were fairly compelled to sheer off, being driven out of the harbour by the pelting of the twenty-four pounder. Some of the crew of the frigate and schooners were wounded, and one of the Maldonadians had his arm shattered by a grape shot.

About six miles from Maldonado is situated the small town of San Carlos, which our party visited, and were received very politely by the Spanish young ladies, who exclaimed, "*Viva los Ingleses,*" and waved their white handkerchiefs, greeting our arrival. On our road back we called in, as usual, at Donna Francisca's, and found a party of Donnas enjoying their "*matté*," which is a sort of herb, put into a small cup, with sugar; hot water is then poured on it, and it is imbibed through a long tube (and some are of silver) at the end of which is a round strainer to prevent the herb getting through; and as it is reckoned a piece of politeness to offer the *matté* to strangers (the ladies first using the tube, and then presenting it to the gentlemen, who must sip some up likewise, but without wiping it,) we were somewhat surprised that it was not offered to us, which Donna immediately perceived, and she said that she had observed "that most English gentlemen were not partial to that Spanish custom;" but we over-ruled this, and all of us had a suck at the hot *matté*, old Donna first preparing the tube, by indulging in a little suction, previous to its being offered to us: I believe it is not generally known that wiping the tube after its having been sucked by any lady is one of the greatest affronts that can be offered them. The greater part of the men at this place wear long knives, stuck in the girdle, on the right side; and boys of a very early age are armed in the same manner. Beef is very cheap, and a bullock may be purchased for a few dollars. Their horses likewise are good; and the Maldonadians are excellent horsemen, and are seldom to be seen without the laço, which is a long thong of leather with a sliding noose at the end of it, and with this they are sure of securing, even when at a full gallop, either horses or bulls, by the head or feet. The Beagle was now ordered to Monte Video, the Adventure remaining at Maldonado, where we arrived without any adventure occurring worth relating.

The inhabitants here, like those of Teneriffe, are not very highly educated. The lower classes indulge themselves in the pleasing pursuit of getting money, and trouble themselves little about any thing else. The mediocre, and particularly the younger part of a family, go slip-shod about the house of a morning, in a glorious dishabille; and the preparation for an evening party will occupy them three or four hours; and the style of dressing their hair, and entwining the roses with a judicious delicacy and taste, to ensure a good effect, is not the least of the difficulty. Upon no consideration will the Spanish female at Monte Video admit a stranger to an interview unless she is prepared to set off the fine symmetry of her figure in an elegant dress and a silk stocking, *couleur de rose*, to display the shape of as pretty an ancle as you would wish to see; while the neat small foot (in a shoe of cerulean blue) chastens the whole appearance. The brilliancy and darkness of their eyes, and the tone of their persuasive guitars, have proved too attractive for many of the young Brazilian officers, who lavish their time and money at this harbour. The introduction to the families of the young senoras is not difficult; and should he chance to be a young man who can make himself generally agreeable in company, and be very fond of singing, he cannot fail of getting himself into an intrigue and a hobble at the same time. However, in Monte Video, the greater number of the Spanish girls are not handsome: Toleta Torres, from Lima, is the belle of the place. I have seen more than one lieutenant walk by her side, on tiptoe, whispering soft expressions, and "sighing like a furnace." I wish her every success, this native of Lima. On the cathedral the marks of the shot are still visible, received during the memorable siege of this place by the British forces; and one of the cupolas is still wanting, having been carried away at the time of the bombardment. The centre aisle is spacious, and many families, with their attendant slaves, are seen piously kneeling before the altar; and it has rather an impressive effect to behold so many persons, in the meridian of life, *couchant* on their carpets, "where the silent circle fan themselves;" but the soft and merry glances of their eyes told plainly enough that they were rather more fond of love and music than the sound of the tinkling bell which is rung by the padré as a signal for all to pray. Without the fan, a Spanish lady would be quite *gauche;* and their manner of using it is one of the most graceful movements imaginable. The silence of the cathedral, and the continual whirring sound occasioned by the opening and shutting of the fan, produces an effect peculiar enough. The jet-black hair of the Donzella, partly concealed from view by the red shawl which gracefully covers her head, is in contrast with the woolly covering which nature has placed on the skull of the slave. The high-minded Donna and the carné seche (dried beef) eating mulatto—the mustachioed Brazilian officer and the steady, scheming, old money-getting Don (who, out of the cathedral, would willingly cut each other's throats) alike squat down, cheek by jowl—their religion reducing them all to an equality in this place. In short, the most wretched and desperate characters that lurk about Monte Video, both male and female, beggars, and the haut ton, are mingled together, presenting a singular assemblage of rags and finery. At the signal given by the padré, all pray most loudly, and strike and beat their bosoms with their fists, in rapid succession. Many cast their eyes upon a favourite saint to invoke protection; and negroes, likewise, solicit the notice of a gaunt black image, placed in a corner of the cathedral. The padré all this time is very busy at the altar, repeating divers prayers, and giving himself a good deal of trouble about the welfare of the souls of those assembled; but more particularly, be it understood, is his attention paid to the young senoras; nor do his assiduity and trouble go unrewarded, for he retires from the fatigue of the morning service to solace himself in the conversation of some of the prettiest girls of the place. There are some highly respectable families in Monte Video; of course it is eligible for those who have daughters ripened into womanhood, to get them married as soon as may be, not only to make room for the younger branches just budding forth, but also to prevent their chances of success being reduced by falling prematurely into the "sere and yellow leaf," which most Spanish ladies generally do after they arrive at twenty-four years of age. The heyday of life with them is between the respective ages of thirteen and twenty-five. They are a heavy supper eating race, and the civility and good-will with which they discuss an olio of turkey, omelet, sweetmeats, salad, oil, and spices, would scare the delicacy of a bread-and-butter-nibbling Miss of the fashionable world. I hope I shall not be accused of harshness towards these young ladies, if I venture a remark upon the general routine of education adopted in most Spanish families; but the innate talent, which they possess in an eminent degree, is not sufficiently cultivated, and a superficial knowledge of the essential branches of education, and a few novels for amusement, embrace the whole extent of their studies. Their passions, either of love or hatred, are intense; and nothing would screen a person from the vengeance of a female, if trifled with. There are not wanting, in Monte Video, many characters who, for a pittance of a few dollars, would speedily carry any revengeful design into effect; and should a person unfortunately cultivate an "honest friendship with a married woman" (as there is no law in force there against crim. con.), his further stay (if discovered) would be extremely unsafe: the *cuchillo* would, some night when he least expected it, find its way to his heart, and satisfy the vindictive temper of the Spaniard by the death of the individual. I can almost venture to pronounce with safety, that out of the many young ladies who enliven the gay Tertulia with their presence, but very few could be found capable of penning a letter; and such is the ruinous system of education pursued even from their earliest childhood, that ere they can well walk, the aged and indolent Aya, who is entrusted with the care of their persons, actually teaches them to lisp the name of the newest Spanish waltz before that of *Nuestra Senora*—that more pains are taken in teaching them dancing and music than any thing else; and certainly they all are accustomed to walk with a singular delicacy of step: and their dress, too, is not neglected, for

> "Curl'd, scented, furbelow'd, and flounced around,
> With feet too delicate to touch the ground,
> They stretch the neck and roll the wanton eye,
> And sigh for every fool that flutters by."
>
> *Cowper.*

They possess the most cheerful tempers, and to a stranger are generally hospitable. Most naval officers find amusement and an asylum at their houses. Without saying much upon their morality, it yet requires a thorough acquaintance before you can venture to offer them the usual attentions of gallantry. Few people are more cautious of strangers; and such is the reserve manifested sometimes on a casual interview, that a person, not accustomed to their manners, would find himself sufficiently uncomfortable when seated among a party of silent young women. On visiting frequently, all this formality is thrown aside, and the whole secret of their character bursts upon you—blindman's buff, forfeits, hunt the slipper, and laughing and waltzing, are the favourite amusements of an evening; and the elderly people are particularly *en avant* in these games, and intermingle their "childish treble" with the jocund sound of the younger, giving an idea of one of Rochefoucault's observations, that

> "Vivacity increased by age, falls little short of frenzy."

In conclusion: as the very soul of a Spanish girl is placed in dancing, music, and singing, it will prove no slight introduction to their favour if you approach them *con amore*. It is advisable never to look serious; and if you cannot speak Spanish, speak in English, or in any language, so that you keep up a continual talk. Never mind the gravity of their countenance, and the having no rejoinder but yes and no for the first five minutes, for when the waltz commences,

> "Seductive waltz, though on thy native shore,
> E'en Werter's self proclaim'd thee half a w—e,"

all formality is thrown aside, and she steps forth a laughing Hebe, and will accompany you through so many dances during the evening, that you may safely reckon, if unaccustomed to them, on a good head-ache in the morning.

The theatre is a most wretched place; the worst of our provincials is better decorated. The benches in the pit are dirty, and partitioned off and numbered, that you may, on paying for your entrance, occupy the same seat in the pit as the one marked on your ticket of admission. The boxes have no seats at all: generally a family or a party take a box among them, but find their own chairs—a difficulty that puzzled the whole of our party, for the practice of bringing chairs we had no idea of. This alarmed our interpreter, a very worthy and intelligent German, much more than it did any of us—the necessity of having such furniture he entirely overlooked till then. "We had better not go into the pit, however," said the German, "it is full of fleas." "Well, we must all go into the gallery." "You must not go there, indeed," said he, "it is full of women; and, besides, they will not allow you to remain, as the gallery is set aside purposely for ladies, and no men are suffered to pass; and if you observe attentively, you will perceive it is as I represent." This I accordingly did, and there were seated a numerous mixture of mulatto, white, and black girls, and each seemed to be in particular good-humour, and their dresses so extremely gaudy, that each might be said to be tinselled and bespangled like any of their saints:—

"but there
All likeness ends between the pair."
Don Juan.

Not being able to procure seats for the boxes, we descended into the pit; and, I believe, felt much less incommoded by the gambols of a few skipping harmless fleas, than by the appearance of many Brazilian mulatto officers attached to the army and navy. They are hated by the Americans, loathed by the Spaniards, spit on by the French, and laughed at by the English; and they seem to be so aware of their own degeneracy, as sincerely to despise and abominate each other. The lower tier of boxes is on a level with the pit, and in these were to be seen some of the handsomest of the Spanish ladies, with the usual display of dark luxuriant hair entwined with roses. The ornaments on the outside of the boxes consist of coloured papers, as variegated as a harlequin's jacket; and the lighting up of the theatre is after the manner of Scowton's show—to one of the beams is affixed a rope, to which is attached a circular piece of wood, containing a galaxy of candles. The musical force of the establishment consists of a few fiddles, a ramping horn, and a drum; and the actress (for they have but one) is about forty years of age, and unfortunately "sans teeth;" however, she possesses a very agreeable lisp, and the manner in which she goes through an evening's performance, which generally consists of a tragedy, dancing, and a farce, proves that she has had some experience in her day. I happened to go behind the scenes one night, and I beheld this Prima Donna sitting upon the knee of one of the actors, indulging in a little "*Aquadente*," but,

> "I protest
> Against all evil speaking, even in jest."
>
> *Don Juan.*

After our return from Monte Video to Maldonado, the Adventure sailed for the former place, but remaining there longer than she had determined upon, we sailed up to join her; and on our passage made our number to H. M. S. Ranger, and soon afterwards fell in with the Adventure about mid-channel. The Adventure had found the English packet (King Fisher) on shore on the English bank, and had succeeded in getting her off. We also met some Brazilian frigates and brigs standing for the island of Goritti, in order to fortify it, and to annoy the Maldonadians by every possible means. We now made all sail along the great coast of Patagonia; and on the 28th of the month, the ships entered the Bay of, and anchored off, Port St.

Elena. Here we found good anchorage for several ships, but it is exposed to a heavy swell from the south-west; this we fully experienced, for a tremendous sea, occasioned by heavy squalls, rolled in upon us and exposed us to the danger of being driven upon the rocks, which lay within a cable's length of us. The surrounding country is of frightful sterility and barrenness; no trace of vegetation can be met with; a universal chaos seems to reign, and nothing can be heard on the land but the harsh cry of the water-fowl and the roaring of the foaming surf on the dark and rugged rocks which line the shore. There is nothing indicative of its having been visited by any human being from the interior, and the whole country for miles round is such a wilderness as would prove most distressing to any crew who were so unfortunate as to be wrecked on this coast. Numerous herds of the wild guanacoe range in undisturbed possession of this trackless waste, and they are so docile as to allow of your near approach, although in some instances it required much manoeuvring to get them within range of the musket. The flesh is rather coarse, but when made into a sea-pie is enticing enough, and particularly after a day's shooting at Port St. Elena, for at this anchorage you meet with no berries or fruits, and, moreover, there is a great scarcity of fresh water, and all the ponds are brackish, and for miles up a sort of marsh it had that taste; this, added to the intolerable heat, and a walk of eight or ten miles, make you glad enough to get on board, and take a libation of "swiggle," where, at your ease, you can d—n the climate, the brackish water, and the long hollow valleys, and also view your cut and swoln lip in the glass of your dressing-case (your messmates laughing all the while), the sad consequence of the recoil of your gun in endeavouring to bring down the guanacoe at a long shot. You here meet the ostrich, and venomous snake, the eight-banded armadillo, and the cavee or fox. Hawks, owls, and buzzards, and various kinds of sea-fowl are the only remaining inhabitants of this wilderness.

From the quantity of wood thrown up high upon the beach, it appeared that a wreck had taken place at this port, but no doubt the survivors had got away from this desolate abode and put to sea. We found a piece of wood pointing out the grave of one of the party, with this inscription (but without date); "John Myers, Armourer, Commodore Decatur, New York," and as time had not made much havoc on this memento, it is probable that the wreck had taken place about five or six years previous to our arrival. We conveyed most of the wreck on board for fuel.

From want of better amusement, some gentlemen of the Adventure set fire to the long dry grass and withered stubble (which covered some acres of ground), and the wind carrying the flames into the deep valleys, raised an immense fire, which spread over the country to a great distance, and blazed away most furiously, making us think very little of the consecrated bonfires we had previously seen blazing in the streets of the city of Rio.

This illumination, we afterwards ascertained, was observed at sea from a distance of fifty miles, and was the only inducement for a cutter, which we had previously fallen in with, to haul in for the land, her captain conjecturing that some casualty had happened to the ships.

One day, on the landing of a shooting party from the Beagle, we perceived three ostriches, and it may be imagined that the ostriches perceived us, for they commenced a sort of trot towards some rising ground which skirted the sea beach, and without turning their heads to see if we were following, disappeared in a moment. On our arrival at the top of the hill, breathless and anxious (for we expected the ostriches to be quietly waiting our arrival on the other side of it), no trace of them was to be seen, and nothing was discernible but a waste of country for miles a-head, although scarcely three minutes had elapsed from the time when we first saw them. We gazed at each other as much as to say, where the devil are they?

The wind having veered to a desirable point, we weighed and made sail on the 4th December. The next land off which we anchored was Cape Fairweather; yet, notwithstanding its inviting name, we experienced severe south-westerly gales, which raged incessantly. This land is not so mountainous as that of Port St. Elena, but from the sea it bears equally as desolate and isolated an aspect. The cape is said to be much like the South Foreland, and the line of coast resembles that of Kent. The country in the distance has a green appearance, but nearer the coast there is plenty of grass, which is burnt and scorched by the influence of the sun. Innumerable herds of guanacoe are to be seen scattered over the distant plains, and they are so tame as to be approached within a few paces. The brown eagles, startled at the appearance of man in this forsaken place, keep incessantly whirling over your head, heedless of shot, and seem inclined to pounce down upon you. The guaguar, or South American tiger, was seen prowling and skulking among the rocks near the beach, but on our approach it quickly made off, sometimes stopping and looking round, and then making away for the interior of the country. From the quantities of bones which lay bleaching in the wind, it would appear that these savage animals continually prey upon the timid and harmless guanacoe. There are quantities of shrubs growing here bearing a red berry; which scent the air to a great distance by their peculiarly sweet and genial fragrance. No vestige of a human being could be met with; and the whole of this part of the coast of Patagonia, from Port St. Elena to Cape Virgins, presents the same cheerless and wild appearance, and in a space of nearly one thousand miles not a tree or bush is to be seen; and the continuation of the land to the northernmost entrance of the Straits of Magellan bears the same bleak and wild aspect. At the time we were off Cape Virgins, a reef was distinctly visible, running out about a mile into the sea. This cape is said to resemble the land off Cape Vincent in Spain.

It was at this anchorage that we first perceived the land of Terra del Fuégo just perceptible above the horizon. The first land that strikes the eye upon entering the straits is a mount, designated "Mount Dinéro," very much in appearance like Monte Video, and about the same size. The next land is Point Possession, which is rather high and bluff, and in this bay the two ships came to anchor on the 19th. We weighed again on the 21st, but meeting with a direct contrary wind, we were obliged to anchor nearer in land, having previously brought up at five or six miles off shore. We remained here several days unsheltered from the prevailing S. W. winds, which blew very severely, and the tide is particularly strong and rapid. Most of the time that we lay here we had a succession of these S. W. gales, accompanied with heavy rain and cloudy weather. On the north side of the bay are four rather conically-shaped mounts, called by Sir John Narborough (one of the preceding navigators), "Amon and his four children," and named also by him "The Ass's Ears," from the resemblance which they certainly bear to the upper part of the head of that animal.. The best anchorage is about two or three leagues from Amon. On our weighing, we found the anchor and cable were as bright as silver, and for these shores the chain-cable is the safest to use. Whilst at this anchorage Christmas-day arrived, and our private stock of provisions was put in requisition to furnish a good dinner in honour of it. What we lacked in fish and flesh we made up in puddings and pies, and our table was amply furnished with such fare; we were all merry and happy, and notwithstanding our being in the Bay of Possession, with a heavy swell on, we had each taken, before two o'clock, a sufficiency of grog to compose us very quietly to sleep. Our next attempt was the passage of the Narrows of the Hope, and this day we had made some way through them; but the prevailing s.w. winds, assisted by a tide running against us at the rate of six or seven miles an hour, compelled us to return into the Bay of Possession. We here again encountered some furious winds, but on the 28th of December we made our second attempt, and with some difficulty accomplished the intricate navigation of the Narrows, having weighed anchor this day at eight o'clock, and we had passed them by eleven. The day preceding our second attempt, a great smoke was visible on the Fuegian shore, apparently a great way inland, but no natives could be perceived through the telescope. The distance between the shores of Patagonia and

Terra del Fuégo, at this Narrow, may be computed at four or five miles, the shores approaching each other nearer at this place than at any other passage of the straits. This land is tolerably high, but not striking or picturesque. The guanacoe at this place are extremely wild, and fled immediately they perceived the ship standing in shore; for, in tacking, to get through the Narrows, we frequently came within a few hundred yards of the land. The smoke of a large fire was now seen on the Patagonian side, but at a considerable distance up the country. The coast, until you arrive at the "Bay of the Thousand Virgins," is not marked by any peculiarity; the highest land is on the southern shore. The coast on the Second Narrows is remarkably bold and rugged, and continues in a line, gradually vanishing into the Bay of Possession. We came-to in the Bay of the Thousand Virgins, having in sight Point St. Gregory and Port San Isidro.

On the 1st of January we again made sail, and anchored in St. Gregory's Bay, in thirteen fathoms, about five or six miles from the Second

Narrows. This is an excellent anchorage, and well sheltered from the prevailing severe winds, which are constantly veering from S.W. to W.S.W. and S.S.W. At this place we saw another great cloud of smoke, appearing at a considerable distance inland. The shore here is more pleasing than any from Cape Virgins, the general appearance of the coast until you arrive here being solitary and gloomy. A long tract of mountain is occasionally seen, covered with heath and verdure; but generally dark and ragged precipices, and overhanging cliffs, destitute of any vegetation, intersect the land on both shores. Captain Stokes and Lieutenant Skyring, the assistant-surveyor, and a midshipman, landed at this bay, with the chronometers, which were left in charge of the middy, while the captain and Lieutenant Skyring proceeded to a rising ground, about a mile distant, for the purpose of making observations. Whilst the midshipman was thus leisurely waiting their return, he perceived a large and savage-looking animal making way towards the place where he stood, snuffing the ground as he came along. This was rather an uncomfortable sight for Llewyllin (a *sobriquet* given him by his messmates), who now commenced quickly loading the musket, which he had luckily brought with him, and by the time this four-footed stranger had arrived within two hundred paces, the middy had fired a shot to make him bring-to. The ball struck not very wide of the mark, but had no other effect than causing the animal to pursue the same manœuvres as the lion was said to have acted towards Don Quixote when that valiant knight waited for him at the open door of his cage. The midshipman now lay down, and resting the musket to steady his aim, the second shot whistled over the head of the creature, who now seemed determined to cultivate a nearer acquaintance, and kept advancing towards him at a quicker rate; but on arriving within fifty paces the third bullet struck the earth close to his head, when he immediately stopped and kept looking at Llewyllin, who ensconced himself in the grass and fired again, when the animal wheeled suddenly round and made off, much in the same leisurely manner as it had approached.

On sailing hence, we fell in with a schooner, which stood in to the bay, and anchored close in-shore: she proved to be the Eliza and Ann, of Stonington, North America, and had been in the Straits some months upon a sealing expedition. The captain of her reported the Patagonian Indians to be friendly (having spoken with them a short time previously), and much inclined to traffic; this piece of information differed very much from the account given by some of his Yankee seamen, who told our men that the natives were exceedingly ferocious, and very much inclined to cut the throats of all strangers, but more particularly of the English; and then followed a tale of a boat's crew from an English vessel having landed upon the coast, some months before, and fired upon the natives, who, in consequence, were determined to murder all who came in their way. All who are acquainted with the Yankees are well aware of their inventive genius; but the captain of the schooner, however, told the truth in saying that the Indians were friendly; and this seemed the more strange, for these precious trading Yankees possess neither honour nor common honesty, nor one single idea beyond the price of cotton and dollars; in fact, our brother Jonathan may be defined to be in character an Englishman grafted on a Jew, as the name we have ingeniously conferred on him evinces—John Nathan.

Towards evening, a large fire blazed forth on the point which extends out of Cape Gregory, and the next morning, two horsemen were seen upon the beach, pacing to and fro, and appeared as if inviting us to land. All on board were now anxious to get on shore, and the more so when we perceived a boat shove off from the Adventure, and proceed in the direction of the Indians. All the telescopes on board were in immediate demand to observe the first meeting with the Patagonians. As the boat neared the land, one of the horsemen came down to the beach, and met the lieutenant, who, on landing, advanced towards him with a musket on his shoulder: the other Indian seemed much more cautious, for, as the boat came close in-shore, he receded about a hundred paces from the other, and there stood with his horse's head turned from the boat's crew, as if doubting whether to remain or go. Captain Stokes now ordered a boat off from the Beagle to land the assistant-surveyor, and in which I was so fortunate as to get a passage. When set on shore, having been landed farther down the bay, I had nearly a mile to walk to the Indians, and on my arrival near the Adventure's boat, the two first that I beheld were a male and female, sitting quietly on a bank, and gazing at a sailor with a musket on his shoulder, who, walking to and fro near them, did not evince less curiosity. The man was apparently about forty-five, and the woman about forty: he was distinguished by a large, broad head, a very smooth face, and angular cheekbones, without either eyebrows or beard; the nose was flat, and the nostrils dilated; the eyes were small, dark, and sunken; the hair was exceedingly black and dishevelled; a small strip of coloured guanacoe skin was bound round the top of the head, confining a single ostrich feather, which waved over his right shoulder, and also partially confined the hair; but notwithstanding this ligature, it hung down on each side of his face, in wild disorder, as low as the breast. The complexion was dark olive, or rather it had a copper-coloured greasy look. He was of a particularly robust make, and about six feet three inches in height; his mouth was remarkably capacious, the lips thick and protruding, and the angles of the mouth contracted excessively, which gave him (notwithstanding a certain vacant stare, which I afterwards observed was peculiar to them all), a ferocity of look not at all inducing a wish for a farther acquaintance; that kind of expression which makes you regret being unarmed. He surveyed me with a peculiar scrutiny, as did the old lady likewise (whom we afterwards heard called by the tribe "Maria"): she seemed to have a much greater share of good-nature than the man, and I therefore offered her a piece of biscuit, which she took between her fore-finger and thumb, and at first nibbled it with all the delicacy and grace of a boarding-school miss; she then became less polite, and crammed her mouth to an overflow.

I did not offer any to the man, and kept my eye upon him to observe if he appeared displeased at the neglect; he seemed to take no notice. I then gave him a few pieces, which he placed very carelessly in the palm of his hand, and whipped them into his mouth in a twinkling. I could not help remarking the facility and satisfaction with which he *cranched* the biscuit. The teeth of both were very even and white, and well calculated to grind the "hard tack," which I had given them, and the noise they both made while thus employed resembled the turning of a coffee-grinder. The old lady at this time smiled very pleasantly, and struck up a tune, her head jogging about as if it had been stuck upon wires. I cannot say "they were the sweetest notes I ever heard," for I did not imagine Nature could be guilty of such wild, incoherent, and unmeaning sounds: she seemed so pleased, that I stepped up to her, and taking hold of her hand, asked her if she could speak Spanish, to which interrogatory she made no reply, but continued her song. On my nearer approach, I found she was not scented, as Don Quixote asks, "like some curious glover," but had, as Sancho Panza observes, "rather a rammish smell," which I found proceeded from an old guanacoe skin in which she was encircled, and a raw piece of young guanacoe, which she seemed to prize very much, as it was fastened by a string close round her naked waist, and concealed under the guanacoe skin, which was her only covering.

I thought this a good chance of taking a sketch of their persons: I accordingly sidled up to the woman, and taking out my sheet of drawing paper, I commenced pencilling her out. The whiteness of the paper attracted their notice very much; they appeared to be a good deal puzzled to account for my looking at them so steadfastly, and then marking the paper. Having commenced upon the old lady Maria, she soon left off singing, and eyed me with great expression and attention; she nevertheless kept up the swinging system with her head, which was continually rolling from one shoulder to the other. The man all this time kept up a continual glib jabber, and I more than once suspected him of "giving lip." I showed him the sketches when I had finished them, at the sight of which his countenance brightened, and turning to the old lady, to my great surprise, he began to laugh, and cried out "*Buéno,*" several times.

At this time the other Indians came galloping up, accompanied by some gentlemen from the Adventure, to whom the above two Indians had lent their horses, which accounted for their remaining behind. The whole group of Patagonians, which now appeared on horseback, consisted of about twenty persons, and among them were several boys and girls; their garb was solely of guanacoe skin, and their countenances had decidedly a Spanish expression. These young savages seemed to understand the system of pillage very well, for I was soon surrounded, and notwithstanding my endeavours to beat them off in the same manner as you would a swarm of bees, it was to no purpose; their curiosity to ascertain what I had in my pockets was irresistible, and I accordingly suffered myself to be quietly robbed of all the tobacco that I had brought with me on shore. The greater number of their countenances appeared feminine, and it required some consideration to determine upon the difference of sex; the general distinction observable was, that the men were broader across the shoulders, and had a sterner expression of countenance; they were all without beards. Among this party there was one in particular who amongst us bore the cognomen of "young Maria;" she was of a fairer hue, and did not possess that disagreeable olive tint. Young Maria seemed to have won the hearts of every one, and very many presents of beads, buttons, and tobacco, were given her; and as a particular mark of distinction, a medal (which had been struck off in England, with the inscription of His Majesty's ships Adventure and Beagle, 1827,) was placed round her neck. Young Maria was always good-humoured, and showed a set of teeth which, for whiteness and uniformity, might have rivalled any in the dentists' shops in May's Buildings. She appeared to recognize the deference paid by the officers to Captains King and Stokes, by her calling them "Capitan;" but there was a wheedling Indian among them, with one eye, who used to style every one "Capitan," particularly when he perceived they had any thing to which he took a fancy.

Most of them were painted above and under the eye with a dark red-coloured earth, others were tinted with a white patch upon the chin and eyebrows. They varied in height from five feet ten inches to six feet three. Some wore buskins, made out of the guanacoe skin, which only came over the foot as far as the instep, leaving the toes bare. Their spurs are of a very curious make; they are each formed of two pieces of wood, about five inches in length, and are placed on the heel like our spur; two pieces of guanacoe skin confine the heel, and keep the sticks about two inches asunder; instead of a rowel, the ends are pointed with sharp iron pins, which project out about two-tenths of an inch. These spurs are confined to the foot by a strip of guanacoe skin, which is attached to the foremost end of each stick, which passes over the instep, and is secured at the ankle.

Round their waists were suspended three long thongs of leather fastened together, having three large balls of granite attached to them, sewed up in hide, and are used for catching wild horses and ostriches. Their method of using them is by holding in the hand one of the balls, whilst the other two are swung round the head until they acquire a certain impetus, they are then thrown at the object; the balls making a rotary motion, entwine round the legs of the pursued horse or ostrich; they are thus thrown down and taken at leisure. Although we had not an opportunity of accompanying them in the chase, yet they showed us the manner of using these "ballas," and also of the "laço," which they also had with them. The women ride astride like the men, and their saddles (for some few had them) are exactly of the same construction as the recádo or recow, consisting of a piece of wood, curved to fit the horse's back (something in the style of the English pack-saddle), with a hole made on each side to admit the stirrup-leather; two or three skins are put over it, and the whole is secured by a broad piece of hide tied under the horse's belly. The bridles are of hide, and the bit is of wood, confined to the horse's head by a strip of guanacoe skin; the stirrups are of a triangular shape, also made of wood, and suspended from the saddle by thongs of hide, of a width only sufficient to admit three toes; the stirrup is generally held with the great toe. Their horses (which are about the size of our ponies) are exceedingly swift; these they generally ride with great rapidity, and lacerate their sides in a dreadful manner (this may be imagined from the construction of the spur, which is, as well as the heel of the buskin, literally covered with blood). As the Adventure's boat, previous to the arrival of Captains King and Stokes, had shoved off, and was proceeding towards the ship, I was left alone among them, and not liking the novelty of my situation, a certain feeling—"valour will come and go,"—induced me to leave the Patagonians, friendly as they were, and proceed at a quick pace towards our own boat. The Indians seeing me running away, and not understanding, I suppose, the reason of my sudden flight, galloped after me. I took this opportunity of placing one of the pistols which were in the boat in the hands of the foremost of them, to see if he had any idea of its use. It appeared to me as if this was the first time he had beheld such a weapon, yet, such is their general apathy, he did not discover any astonishment; neither had he any idea of discharging it, for when I placed his finger upon the trigger he did not offer to pull it, and on my pulling it for him, he did not manifest the least fear at the novelty of the report. The boat being about to return to the ship, I gave them some buttons, and taking "my last look and farewell of Maria," was soon alongside the Beagle. I was told by the assistant-surgeon, that during my absence three or four Patagonians had been rowed off to the ship, and the *nonchalance* and unconcern which they showed while on board were laughable enough; one of the party, about six feet in height, and distinguished from the rest by a long straight nose, kept lolling against one of the guns and whistled away very unconcernedly; they all gave a proof of the apathy of their temper, for they took little or no notice of any thing during their stay in the ship. I shall here take my leave of them for the present,

"by and by I'll prattle,
Like Roland's horn in Roncesvalles battle."

Some of the Patagonians were persuaded to go on board the Adventure, and proceed with her as far as a certain point, where they were to be landed. At noon this day, the tide favouring us, we weighed and made sail for the second Narrows, formed by the Island of Nassau and Cape Gregory, which we had passed by two P.M.; these Narrows are about thirteen miles in length, by four or five in breadth; the Spanish navigators have given to them the appellation of St. Simon; the English that of St. Bartholomew's. At five P.M. we anchored under the east end of Elizabeth Island, and, on looking towards the shores of Patagonia, an immense smoke covered the whole extent of coast, the Patagonian tribes having followed the vessels towards the point where their companions were to be landed. Elizabeth Island is rather high and rugged, yet very level on the top; there are no trees upon it, but green verdure covers the surface in many places: we lay all the night and the following day under the lee of the island, as it blew very hard from the S.W. On the 5th of January we got under weigh, with a westerly wind, which was favourable for passing between Elizabeth and Penguin Islands, commonly said to be the most dangerous passage known in the straits; we soon passed Elizabeth Island, and at Black Point (Point Negro) the Indians on board the Adventure were set on shore. About this place the woody country commences, and the coast down to Fresh-water Bay is so thickly covered with trees, and presented such a contrast to the barren and arid wastes which we had hitherto seen, that the eyes of each on board seemed refreshed by viewing these thick forests which impenetrably grew upon the sides of the high mountains. Many hundreds of trees had been torn up by the wind, and scattered along the beach. At Fresh-water Bay, which is on the Patagonian coast, there is a very open roadstead, but a tolerably good anchorage about one mile and a half off shore; great quantities of excellent-flavoured geese, ducks, teal, and snipe are to be met with in the various ponds which skirt the beach; and the geese are the largest and most curiously feathered of any in the straits.

The breast is entirely covered with small black feathers, thickly studded with white spots; they weigh from eight to ten pounds: I believe these to be the Brant geese mentioned by Sir John Narborough. Towards the evening of the last day that we remained here, a party of seven Fuegians came round a point in their canoes.

As these were the first natives of Terra del Fuégo that we had seen, a short description of them may be interesting. They are of small stature, the tallest among them not being more than five feet two inches, and all of them, both male and female, were in a most destitute condition; the seal-skin, which comprises their only covering, fluttered in miserable tatters around their swarthy and greasy bodies; their coarse black hair, having the appearance of split whalebone, hung over their face and shoulders, and it is hardly possible to conceive human beings in a more wretched and degraded condition: they greedily devoured some rancid seal blubber.

Leaving this wandering tribe to the full enjoyment of their unctuous fare, we again got under weigh and stood towards Port Famine, which was the next anchorage we were destined to touch at. The coast from Fresh-water Bay to Port Famine presents the same appearance, nothing but impervious forests; the land is not very high, the Fuegian coast being scarcely perceptible from the Patagonian shore. We encountered on our passage down to Port Famine some extremely heavy squalls, and the crew appeared much rejoiced when we cast anchor in this harbour on the 6th of January. The land here is higher than any we had previously seen. The name of Port Famine was given to this place by one of the former navigators, in consequence of a settlement having been formed here by the Spaniards in 1584; and out of four hundred persons, only three or four had survived, the remainder having been literally starved to death. The Barberry tree is found here in great quantities, and also the Arbutus, but scarcely any other vegetable production. An exhaustless supply of muscles and limpets may be obtained, but the former are not of that large size which Byron states to have found here. This is a most excellent port either for wood or water; towards the upper end of the bay (S.W.) there are incalculable quantities of large trees, which, seem to have been whitening in the wind for ages, some completely rotten, and others in good preservation; in short, the ground all around is so thickly occupied by them, that you are led to wonder where they could all come from. The short time the Beagle remained here, all (whose duty did not keep them on board) were anxious to get on shore to provide for the mess, it having been "banyan" with us, in certain points, a good while; sometimes we supplied ourselves with a few teal, yet we were not always so successful, and as a little privation had made us not over nice in our eating, we sometimes brought on board two or three red beaks, (a dark bird about the size of a pigeon, with a red beak about four inches in length, and a strong fishy smell,) which, with a few parrots, we made into a curry, and thus dined very sumptuously off "pretty poll," our necessities frequently obliging us to pop some of the birds intended as "specimens" into the saucepan. Besides the birds before mentioned, we here found kingfishers, (a pretty curry,) goss-hawks, vultures, hawks, different species of owls, various kinds of sea-gulls, blackbirds, and thrushes, and a singular kind of small owl, with a variety of smaller birds; fish in abundance, the Adventure's seine having taken a miraculous draught; some of the smelts were of an extraordinary size and brilliancy, weighing upwards of three pounds each.

This life was too good to last long; the 15th of January arrived, and orders were sent on board the Beagle for parting company, when, taking leave of our friends on board the Adventure, the Beagle unmoored, and at six o'clock, A.M. had sailed out of Port Famine to proceed upon a survey of the western entrance of the Straits of Magellan, leaving our consort safely moored at Port Famine; and, as orders had been given for fitting their yawl as a cutter, for a survey of the opposite side of the coast about Port Valdez, we did not doubt when we met again, that "we should each have a tale to tell." The weather was fine, but hazy, and at eight A.M. Point St. Anne was bearing N.W. ¾ W,

Cape Shut Up of Byron, or San Isidro of the Spaniards, S. ½ W. Having made St. Nicholas Bay, we anchored in twelve fathoms near a small island within three cables' length of us. At a short distance from us, there was another small island of about eighty yards in circumference, covered with trees, upon which were perched numbers of birds; we were not long in pulling towards them, but on our near approach they turned out to be our old friends the "shags," and of course not worth shooting at. The assistant-surgeon here shot the first white goose, and not without some concern did we leave behind us a nest of little ducks, they being too young for a curry. The surgeon, purser, and master proceeded to a river, which runs up into the country thick with woods and swamps, but they did not meet with a single bird. This is not a safe place to run into in foul weather, the anchorage being so precarious; the impervious woods and the surrounding country are desolate to look upon, and here reigns a thorough isolation—every thing silent and dreary.

On Tuesday the 17th, being becalmed, our

boats were sent out to tow, but soon afterwards a breeze springing up, we up boat, and made all sail; on the evening of the 18th, after tacking and sounding many times during the day, we were sheltered under Cape Holland. This cape is very high and bluff, and here the Fuegian shore begins to wear a desolate and chilly aspect. The mountains which skirt the beach are of extreme height; those inland are still higher, and covered with snow; and when the weather sets in hazy and tempestuous, which is often the case, it forms no very pleasing look-out. In lying under Cape Holland you have a shingly anchorage, and are tolerably sheltered from the prevailing S. W. winds; the Patagonian coast (about here) is frightfully mountainous and woody, and the channel nearly five or six miles in width. On the 20th we were off Cape Forward, likewise a high bluff promontory; the beach is covered with thick woods and trees, which grow nearly to the tops of the mountains; the land in the interior is of great altitude, and covered with a perpetual snow. It blew very fresh at the time we were passing this cape, and the squalls off the land came on so suddenly as to require much vigilance and care to prepare for them. We met with little really tempestuous weather on our passage from thence to Port Gallant, where we safely anchored in four fathoms. This is one of the best and safest harbours in the Straits, affording a safe and ready mooring, entirely land-locked, and sheltered from all winds. There is a long narrow spit, or sand, which rises from the mouth of a small river on the northern shore, and extends about one-third across the harbour. The anchorage is of strong dark blue mud. As soon as our ship got into the harbour, which lies nearly east and west, she was brought to, both on account of the sand-bank, and the wind being dead on end, and warped up a few cables' lengths in order to be perfectly secure.

Whilst lying here I read the following passage in Captain Wallis's Narrative of his Voyage through the Straits of Magellan, in 1767: "In Port Gallant Bay," he says, "the master of the Swallow climbed one of the highest mountains, which are here very lofty, hoping from the summit he should obtain a sight of the South sea, but he found his view interrupted by mountains still higher on the southern shore; before he descended, however, he erected a pyramid, within which he deposited a bottle containing a shilling and a paper, on which was written the ship's name and the date of the year; a memorial which possibly may remain there as long as the world endures." One of the midshipmen received an order from Captain Stokes to ascend in search of it, one of the mountains which appeared most practicable, being free from thickets, and unlike the others by which we were surrounded, which were thick and intricately wooded to their summits, and nearly four thousand feet in height. I obtained leave to accompany him; we proceeded in our search, after continuing which for a length of time with as much perseverance as ever was manifested by "Christian" in the "Pilgrim's Progress," we began to wonder whereabout the "Master" had erected the "Pyramid," and not finding it, we concluded we must have mistaken the mountain; we therefore retraced our steps and arrived on the beach in a wet and muddy condition, disappointed in not finding the "bottle," or meeting with any "specimens," except a poor twittering swallow which we shot at the highest part of the mountain.

Dr. Bowen having suggested (the next day) the probability of discovering the bottle on some of the other mountains, which were of a still greater altitude, I volunteered to accompany him in a second search; so taking with us a gun and a pint-bottle of brandy, we soon entered the brakes which skirt the base of the mountain. Dr. Bowen proceeded first, and, being a tall athletic man, he broke down the interwoven thickets, so that I was enabled to proceed with less difficulty. About four hundred yards up the mountain the acclivity became much steeper, and at every step we sank above our knees in withered stubble and moss; in this manner we proceeded, almost in darkness, from the thick foliage of the trees, until we were stopped by a huge rock, which, jutting out, cut off all possibility of ascending farther in that direction, unless we had a mind to mount in the style of the "futtock shrouds," which was not the doctor's *forte* any more than my own. We then determined to round this part of the mountain, and here found a less objectionable passage. With much difficulty we ascended a considerable distance, our path being continually obstructed by decayed roots of trees, till we arrived at another fearful projection, along the edge of which we could perceive an opening of about thirty yards in length, which led to a part of the mountain altogether divested of trees. Dr. Bowen went fearlessly forward, and I could do no less than follow him; but he excelled me both in courage and speed, and I soon lost sight of him. I then had recourse to bawling out his name, and the sound of his voice gave me that kind of confidence which I should suppose a person would feel when suddenly buried alive, on hearing the voices of persons employed in digging him out. Having got through this passage, a few paces brought me to the top of the mountain, and I was now upon a level plain, where several small ponds had formed, beside one of which was seated Dr. Bowen, dipping some biscuit in the crystal water; this reminded me of the player (Melchor Zapata) whom Gil

Blas encountered in his journey "soaking crusts of bread in a spring." We took this opportunity of drinking the brandy, and also of looking down upon the Beagle, which appeareded about half her tonnage. At the distance of nearly a quarter of a mile, we perceived a conically shaped mountain, upon which we expected to find our prize; so, surmounting a very great inclination to sleep, I arrived soon after the doctor at the top of this first conic elevation; but here was no pyramid, nor any indication of there ever having been one; we then proceeded to a still higher cone of the mountain about 500 paces from where we stood, and there was the "pyramid," (not quite so large as those of Egypt, for this was only four feet in height,) and, on removing the stones we perceived a bottle, broken in halves, in which was the "shilling," and several of what appeared to be musket cartridges, in a very damp condition: around the base of the pyramid were scattered several pieces of decayed wood; these were carefully collected, and taking the shilling and cartridges, we wrote, with a pencil, on a piece of paper, the following notable certification, as far as my memory serves: "Dr. Bowen and Mr. Macdouall, of his Britannic Majesty's ship Bèagle, Pringle Stokes, Esq. commander, visited this spot in January, 1827, and found a bottle containing a shilling and several cartridges. They have left a pint bottle, in which was placed an English shilling and several buttons." Having enclosed this paper with an English shilling (which was compressed nearly double in order to admit of its entrance) in the empty brandy bottle, we replaced the old bottle, placed ours by its side, rebuilt the pyramid, and prepared to return.

On looking towards the sea-shore we perceived there was little or no impediment by this side of the mountain, there being scarcely any trees or bushes, in comparison with those we had encountered on the side by which we had ascended; and we should have chosen it for our descent, but, calculating that on reaching the sea-shore we should be, from the windings and deep lagoons which are visible along the line of coast, at least eight or ten miles from the ship, we returned as we went, and with much less difficulty. On our arrival on board we made Captain Stokes acquainted with the success of our expedition, and deposited in his hands the cartridges and the shilling. A day or two afterwards it was reported that what we had supposed cartridges, were memorials! but of their purport we could discover nothing until our return to Port Famine (two months afterwards), when they were presented to Captain King. They were then ascertained to be Bourgainville and Cordoba's memorials of their voyage, the former of date 1766, the other 1786; the memorial left by the master of the Swallow had consequently escaped our search. I shall here take the opportunity of stating, that it was the intention of Captain Stokes to have replaced the shilling and the memorials, and to have rebuilt the cross placed here by Cordoba (*Morro do Cruz*, Port Gallant), of which the decayed wood seemed to have been a part, on his return to the straits for the second survey.

Leaving Port Gallant on or about the 21st January, Captain Stokes, in his haste to get through the straits, had forgotten to take on board several of the boarding-pikes which had been arranged along-shore, and to which were affixed silk handkerchiefs, for the purpose of survey. They were consequently left there, though he intended to remove them on his return to the harbour. We moved on to the westward, occasionally encountering those heavy squalls off the land which blow with such an overwhelming force from the south-west. Smoke was visible on both shores, but we did not bring-to to speak the natives. The line of coast from Cape Notch to Cape Providence, on both shores, presents a chain of snow-capped mountains rising to a great height; intermingled among them are dark cavities of rocks, others rising in conical shapes, and forming a thousand different figures, which, with the trees and forests occasionally breaking upon the sight, give some idea of the wilderness in this part of the world. Having anchored under Cape Providence, we found it to be tolerably good holding ground, but rather a dangerous harbour to run into, particularly in squally or foggy weather, as there are various rocks visible just above the water.

We had now passed a stretch of country of nearly two hundred and fifty miles, the wind having been directly contrary the whole distance. The almost incessant rain and damp and cold atmosphere began to have its effect upon our crew, and some of our strongest and most able-bodied seamen were fast sinking under a constant exposure upon deck, which continued gales of wind made absolutely indispensable. To particularise the daring and determined attempts made for the last few days by Captain Stokes to reach Cape Pillar (then about thirty-five miles from us) would be perhaps a tedious narration of gales of wind blowing with unrelenting fury right a-head, and only to be appreciated by those who have been beating to windward at the mercy of a heavy sea and the wind blowing a perfect hurricane. Neither was Captain Stokes of a disposition to lay quietly under Cape Providence waiting for fair weather; he was none of your "fair weather Jacks;" but with a resolution and energy hardly to be surpassed, he boldly and fearlessly braved the difficulties which thickened around him; trusting to himself, and having confidence in the skill and seamanship of Lieutenants Skyring and Sholl and the other officers, he vainly endeavoured to reach the western entrance, and was constantly driven back, exposed as we then were to the heavy swell of the great Pacific, which rolled in upon us with unabated violence. After repeated and unavailing trials, Captain Stokes, apparently tired out by the constant and never-varying point from which such heavy squalls set in, determined at all hazards to reach Cape Pillar, and, on the morning of the 31st January, the wind howling around us, and the atmosphere dense and cheerless, we put to sea. During the day we tacked nearly thirty times, and when within ten miles of Westminster Island, the wind blew with redoubled violence. The evening began to close in: still we dashed on, and still were driven back; the sea broke over the vessel many times, and she laboured very much, and oftentimes was buried in the deep trough of the sea. At length we were struck on the larboard side by a heavy sea, which threw us nearly on our beam-ends, the hammock-nettings on the larboard side, towards the forecastle, being completely under water, and the men who were there immersed above their knees: it broke the stanchions and carried away the first gig. The "idlers," who were battened down (and more than ten men were upon the sick-list), seemed to be quite unconcerned at the din and noise overboard—"nothing so much the spirit calms as rum and true religion;"—but talked over the probability of reaching Cape Pillar on such a boisterous evening. By this time it was nearly dark, and nothing was to be seen around us but black and gathering clouds, from which a vivid gleam of lightning occasionally shot, making the gloom still more awful;

> "That night, a child might understand,
> The Deil had business on his hand."

and now Captain Stokes, despairing of making any farther way, ordered "about ship" and ran for our old anchorage: in passing too near the rocks (which I before mentioned are in the harbour), the ship struck three successive times, grating harshly against them, and heeling-over fearfully; each shock made sad defalcations in the glass and crockery, both of the officers and ship's company. At this crisis, nothing could exceed the surprising activity of the sick, particularly of old Baptiste, the black cook, "a gentlemanly kind of man," who, jumping out of his hammock, made directly for the main hatch, loudly vociferating, "God b—t! she go to hell! You tiefs, why you no butt up de hatch?" which being very soon accomplished by those on the doctor's list, up they went, "*sauve qui peut.*" I must not forget to mention one elderly gentleman on board, who had been *estropié* for some time, occasioned by an old ulcer, but who was now seen practising a quick hobble about the gun-room, full of "*dolens mæste,*" looking very pale. I must here beg to digress, and request the learned reader to remember, that if, like Sancho, "I speak a great deal of nonsense, it does not proceed from malice but infirmity," therefore, leaving him ejaculating pious exclamations, and repeating the creed, which, no doubt, he did very incorrectly "in his confusion," I, with some others, rushed upon deck to see what was the matter. The men were all abroad, scarcely knowing which rope to lay hold of; but the danger had been momentary; the fore-sail having been kept on, had dragged her completely over the rocks, and in a few minutes afterwards we were safely anchored. This was what I afterward heard called "touch and go," and, perhaps, one of those occurrences which serve people to talk and laugh about when the danger is past; but, at the time such a mistake really occurs, the case is found to be no laughing matter.

The next morning, the 1st of February, Captain Stokes, accompanied by Mr. Flinn, the master, Mr. Jones, volunteer of the second class, and twelve men, being victualled for five days and well armed, proceeded in the cutter to look out for harbours, so that if we were again assailed by these tremendous squalls we might obtain a nearer shelter than by returning to Cape Providence. The weather had not cleared up; it rained incessantly, and it was, moreover, exceedingly cold; consequently the search upon which the captain had gone did not promise either comfort or enjoyment. The 2d, 3d, 4th, and 5th days had passed, and nothing of the cutter had been heard of, and many conjectures were formed as to her fate. Considerable anxiety was manifested, and many on board unhesitaingly predicted the loss of the whole party. On the afternoon of the 6th day all eyes were strained towards the point where we expected the cutter to appear, and we were about surrendering our last hope of again seeing her, when, to our great joy, she hove in sight, coming down right before the wind. On her arriving alongside, we soon perceived an alteration in the looks of all, except Captain Stokes and Mr. Flinn, who appeared none the worse for the cruise; but, on looking after our messmate, he presented such a whimsical appearance that we scarcely could suppress the laugh to which we felt a strong inclination, for his face, naturally bluff, was puffed up and swollen, and speckled of a blue tint, something resembling that of a drowned person. The effect of the weather upon some of the men had been different: their faces looked as long as an eight shilling teaboard. It was useless for us to ask any questions of Mr. Jones until he had attended to the demands of the "Victualling department;"

one of us was obliged to cut up the provision for him, his hands being rendered nearly powerless from the effects of the cold. The relation which he gave of their cruise proved their having suffered severely; it had rained without cessation the whole time, which prevented them from making a fire, and they were without the possibility of getting a dry shelter, as they found most of the places upon which they landed complete swamps; they were consequently compelled to lie down shivering in their wet clothes, under such shelter as they could find; if so fortunate as to fall asleep, it was but of short duration: they awoke in agony, the wet and damp ground filling them full of "aches and pains." They availed themselves of every short interval of fair weather, and found some good anchorages. Having put into "Separation Harbour," they found there a family of the wandering natives of Terra del Fuégo, consisting of two men and two young children, likewise a dog; the women had been concealed. The elder of the two was a very facetious gentleman, and imitated all he saw done; if spoken to, he repeated the words with a surprising precision, and even the tone and gesture. The captain said to the younger savage, "D—n your eyes, pull off my boots!" which he repeated with the exactness of an echo: he had a particular wish to abscond with any thing that he laid his hands on: a tin can and a spoon he concealed under his seal-skin covering. The children were pretty, and of an interesting tawny colour.—This account made us anxious to weigh from Cape Providence, and bring up in Separation Harbour; but Captain Stokes not having completed the survey, we did not leave it until the 9th February, when, the weather being fine, but still blowing hard, we got under weigh, and after putting into various anchorages, and surveys being made in the boats of many lagoons, coves, and deep bays, on both shores, we arrived at Separation Harbour on the 15th February. It presented on all sides a hideous track of rocks of great altitude, and a perfect wilderness and desolation reigned around us.

At the first opportunity, I succeeded in obtaining a passage on shore, in company with

Dr. Bowen and Lieutenant Sholl, and, on the boat passing the wigmas which was built on the left of the harbour, we beheld, thrust through the top of it, the head and naked shoulders of the younger savage, who loudly cried out *Che-ree-cow-wow, Che-ree-cow-wow,* and these words he continued to bawl out with the whole strength of his lungs. We landed a few minutes afterwards at the farther end of the harbour (where plenty of good water descends from the rocks), and made our way over sharp-pointed rocks to the place they had chosen for erecting the wigwam. When our party came within twenty paces of them we perceived the old Indian, apparently about fifty years of age, standing with a club raised over his shoulder in an offensive position, and a youth of nineteen, with a long straight stick or lance, which he held in the attitude of throwing at us; seeing us stop, they both indulged in a long hideous guttural vociferation, the harsh and inharmonious tones of which savoured more of the growl than the voice of a human being. Having listened patiently to this strange clatter, we again moved forward, our noses forewarning us of an approach towards the Den of Cacus. The old Indian had lowered his club as we came up, and on our giving him a biscuit, he greedily began to gnaw it, holding it fast with both his hands, and calling out *cheop, cheop,* several times. This, we afterwards found out, was a favourite word of his, the meaning of which we vainly endeavoured to ascertain. As he stood close to the entrance of the wigwam, we offered to move him on one side in order to go in, when he again set up his guttural talk, and exclaimed *petites, petites,* and pointed inside the wigwam, to the opening of which we saw come forward two little girls, in a state of nudity, the eldest about the age of six, the youngest four, who both began to cry at the sight of us: but, giving to each a string of white beads and a piece of biscuit, they both ceased crying, and old Che-reecow-wow immediately left off gnawing the biscuit, and set up the cry of *cheop, cheop,* upon which Lieutenant Sholl offered him a string of red ones, which he no sooner beheld than he clutched them with considerable force, and in a moment hid them under his arm-pit. The elder child had its head encircled with a peculiar string of light-coloured small shells, and it was some time before we could persuade the infant to part with them; but the display of some party-coloured beads and a spoon was too much for old Che-ree-cow-wow; he took the shells off the head of the child, but not without first consulting its inclination, (for they appeared to be very affectionate to their children, as we observed in several instances,) and, placing it in the hands of Dr. Bowen, made a vigorous clutch at the spoon and beads, which he deposited in the usual hiding place, uttering *cheop, cheop,* with great eagerness and good-humour. The younger was constantly repeating the words he heard with great accuracy, and also busied himself in attempts to pluck out our eyebrows; it so happened, that he took Lieutenant Sholl off his guard, and gave him a severe twinge. It would appear from this circumstance, and their not having any themselves, that they pluck out their own.

We now all had a dance together, our new

acquaintances jumping about and making as much noise as any of us: and the dirty copper-coloured appearance of the elder Indian struck me, while he thus capered about, as being particularly hideous. He was about five feet six inches in height and exceedingly robust and bread-chested, but had altogether a most miserable appearance; he certainly resembled a devil more than a human being. Having exercised ourselves sufficiently, both the Indians crept upon their hands and knees into the wigwam, the entrance to it being so near the ground as not to allow of any other mode of ingress;—and perhaps it may be as well, for the edification of those who never read of, or saw any, to give some account of these temporary habitations. A great number of long straight branches of trees are fixed in the ground in a circle, at certain distances apart, the area being about fifteen feet; some pliant twigs keep the ends of the branches together, which being bent, form a centre at the top; it is rendered comfortably warm and air-tight by a covering of boughs and seal-skins; the fire is made in the centre, around which they sat in the midst of smoke, which could not possibly escape, there being no aperture at the top, but through the doorway, which being so low, rendered its egress almost impossible; but they appear to be very little incommoded by it. Having thus thrust ourselves into the wigwam, we found our friends huddling over the fire, which now burnt very brightly, and keeping the children close to them; they motioned us to sit down likewise, and we arranged ourselves accordingly. They commenced rummaging about the sides of the wigwam, and soon produced some large muscles, which they put into the fire, and while these were cooking, they extended their limbs and drew closer to the blaze. Not much relishing a farther continuance in the wigwam, we crawled out; and seeing us about to depart, they pointed to the masts of the ship, visible above the headland, and exclaimed *sheroo, sheroo,* by which we understood them to mean the ship, and we beckoned the elder to follow; he pointed to the masts, repeating their word *sheroo,* and came with us some way down the mountain; we then gave him a biscuit to encourage him, but he no sooner received it, than he suddenly changed his mind, and made his way quickly back, waving his hand to bid us farewell as he ran along, repeating the word *sheroo* as long as we were in sight. As the boat passed the wigwam on our return, they both shouted *che-ree-cow-wow*, and continued to utter those words until a turning in the land hid us from their view.

On visiting the shore the day following, and taking with us a good supply of grog and biscuit, we were so fortunate as to crawl into the wigwam just as its inhabitants were at dinner; they had gathered an immense quantity of limpets and muscles, which they were roasting with great dispatch. Having seated ourselves, the younger Indian displayed a characteristic trait of preference to the mid who accompanied our party, by attempting to pluck out his eyebrows; then taking one of the largest muscles that appeared sufficiently roasted, and giving it a turn or two in his mouth, apparently for the purpose of cooling it, he presented the dainty morsel to my companion, who very politely signified his rejection of the proferred favour by shaking his head; the Indian then transferred the muscle to the hand of the elder child, who brought and held it up to our middy's mouth, at the same time talking to him very prettily in Fuegian; but all was quite useless; neither her persuasions nor mine could induce him to venture on a taste. Old Cheop, perceiving my eyes water from the effects of the smoke, immediately dried them with his dirty fist; for this piece of kindness I gave him a button, which he directly hid between his toes, as he did likewise another given him by my friend. Being now anxious to get him off to the ship, I endeavoured by taking hold of my trowsers and other signs to acquaint him, that by going on board he would obtain similar ones; and farther to encourage him, I took off my old flushing jacket and put it upon him. These efforts not availing, I drew forth the bottle of grog, at the sight of which he commenced a rattling noise in his throat. I then placed my hand over his eyes, and held the bottle to his mouth, when he swallowed the liquor greedily; before removing my hand from his eyes, I put the bottle in my pocket; when he found it gone, he made eager signs for more, crying out *cheop, cheop*, and uttering other wild and incoherent sounds. The younger Indian stood by all this time, looking up to the sky, with his hands together above his head, and kept calling out *picharee, picharee*, in a piteous tone of voice, but what he meant I could not possibly make out; however, I comforted him also by a taste of the grog, which he gulped down with equally as much *goût* as the elder and we heard no more about *picharee*. Having by this time gained their entire confidence, I moved down the mountain, inviting the elder Indian to follow, which he did immediately; the younger one, taking his station at the door of the wig-wam (as if to guard the children), cried out, "D—n your eyes," an expression he had picked up amongst us, and of which he was perfect master. To prevent the elder Indian from running back, as he had done the day before, we kept him before us: he made his way down the rocks much easier and swifter than we could, although he was barefooted. On arriving at the boat, we bundled him in, one of the sailor's first helping him on with an old pair of canvass trowsers. We were soon alongside the ship, and he made his appearance, no doubt for the first time, on board of a man-of-war. He evinced a much greater share of curiosity than the Patagonians; he looked around him with much earnestness, gazing sometimes down upon the deck, then up at the rigging, but always kept a look-out to see if I was near him. Captain Stokes ordered him a glass of port wine, which he appeared to like as well as the grog, and finished a second and third glass with great composure of countenance. The doctor, upon this occasion, placed his hand on the top of the Indian's head, to discover if he possessed (as he said) "the organ of veneration;" upon which Old Cheop began to pull and rub the doctor's head likewise, in rather a less unceremonious manner. We soon afterwards introduced him to the "middies' berth," and it being then about four o'clock (our tea-time), we placed before him a basin of warm souchong, made very sweet, into which he immediately put his greasy hand,

and he did not seem inclined to withdraw it, until some of us moved the basin, and placed his hands on either side of it, when he raised it to his mouth and drank the whole off. He now refused to take more grog, but observing him eyeing the sugar, we placed a quantity of it before him; on tasting it, his eyes glistened with delight, while he testified the greatest gratification by sucking and licking his fingers: he now pointed to the basin for more tea, which was given to him until he had emptied it six times; he then fell-to upon some ship's beef and biscuit, which, with a large piece of plum-duff, he very soon conveyed down his throat; but, while thus gloriously stuffing himself, he did not forget the children, for he occasionally placed pieces of beef and pudding under his jacket, next his skin, as he said, for the *petites*. But what he appeared to relish full as much as the pudding, was several "purser's dips" which we gave him; these he finished with an evident "gust," swallowing cotton and all. The candles, however (to use a nautical phrase), "choked his luff:" we then made him a tumbler of very sweet grog, which he drank off, scraping up with his finger the undissolved sugar that had settled at the bottom of the glass. Whilst he was thus agreeably engaged, he contrived to secrete every spoon upon the table; some he placed under his arms, and others up his sleeve. We then gave him a small looking-glass, in which he surveyed himself very steadfastly, and turned the glass to observe what was on the other side, and not seeing his face, he turned it round again, and was a good deal puzzled when he again saw himself; however, he continued to gaze on, till raising his head, and putting on a most ludicrous smile, he looked attentively at every one in the berth, indulging, at the same time, in a low murmuring gabble, which at length burst out into *cheop, cheop,* and suddenly hid the glass in the usual depository, exclaiming *petites, petites,* and huddled himself up, as if fearful of having it taken away from him. I showed him some drawings of the Patagonians, but he did not seem to recognise them. The time having arrived when it became advisable to put him on shore, I made an attempt to recover my flushing-jacket, but he had concealed under it such an olio of beef, pudding, sugar, candles, and biscuit, that it was prettily bedaubed, nor was he at all inclined to relinquish it. Before placing him in the boat, we stuck on his head a red night-cap, so that he looked like a large ourang-outang; we also made him presents of beads, spoons, and knives, with all of which he was highly pleased. As he went on shore, he amused himself (as was reported) by eating the arming of grease off one of the sea-leads employed in sounding.

On the following day, the younger Indian, on perceiving the boat making towards the shore, set up the cry of *che-ree-cow-wow*, and made his way down to the party with great celerity, running over the rocks with a surprising swiftness, and took his seat in the boat, where he waited very patiently until they pulled off to the ship; on being brought into the berth, and the door closed, he displayed great uneasiness, hammering with his hands until it was opened: we treated him in the same manner as we had the elder Indian, but he proved not so voracious a feeder. Before coming on board, he had painted his nose and face; his eyes, which were small and black, did not want lustre; and had it not been for his coarse ragged hair, which hung down the sides of his head and face in lank and dishevelled masses (except over the front of the head, where it was cut smooth, and just long enough to conceal a forehead "villanous low"), he would have looked like a Spanish youth. His features were regular; his wide mouth was well furnished with teeth as white as ivory, and his hands and feet were small and well formed. As he had come on board only with the seal-skin covering, we rigged him out in a flannel waistcoat and shirt, and one of the marines gave him an old red jacket and a pair of canvass trowsers, so that he looked a respectable member of society, and giving him also presents of beads, knives, and looking-glasses, he departed equally pleased and delighted as the elder Indian.

The next day being out on a shooting-party, we paid a visit to the wigwam; the Indians no sooner heard us coming through the bushes, than they ran out to meet us, the younger Indian resumed his tattered seal-skin, and Old Cheop appeared in "cuerpo," with the shirt and flannel waistcoat torn in pieces, rolled round his middle. On entering the wigwam, we saw nothing of the rest of the clothing that had been given to them, except the red cap. After much trouble we succeeded in obtaining some spear heads, made probably from the bones of the seal and otter; also some shells, which serve them to drink out of, and likewise several wicker baskets of a rude construction. We could not ascertain the method they used to obtain fire, and in order to discover it, we were about to extinguish the one they had in their wigwam, but no sooner did they perceive our intention, than they rushed in to prevent us, and appeared so earnest that we deemed it prudent to desist. Around their hut were scattered a great quantity of muscle and limpet shells and seal-bones; they use the club to kill the latter animal, as we discovered by pointing to that weapon, when the elder Indian struck the ground several times, and pointed to the sea, at the same time blowing and snuffing, as if to give us an idea of the noise made by the seals. At this time the younger made an attack upon the eyebrows of Mr. Bynoe, using a muscle-shell as a pair of tweezers. We left them soon afterwards, and saw them no more. They were building a canoe while we were with them; it was formed of several pieces of some kind of bark, along the edges of which were made several holes, and fastened or sewed together with seal-gut. Nature seems to have endowed these people with much ingenuity and perseverance, for the labour required to build these canoes must be very great, sharp muscle-shells being their only implements. Among the variety of trees which compose the woods at this harbour, the birch is the largest, growing to from twenty-five to twenty-six feet in height, but generally very crooked; in the building of small vessels it might be rendered serviceable. The winter bark (of which there is an abundance) is distinguished by its leaves resembling those of the laurel; it grows very straight, and is in height about thirty feet, the dimensions rarely exceed twenty inches, and the square nine or ten. There are also other bushes, bearing a white blossom, eight or ten feet high, of a singular hardness; and also the Barberry tree, whose stem and branches are of a warped and irregular growth, and there are no other trees of size, in the woods at this anchorage, worthy of attention or remark.

On the 20th of February we again got under way, and came-to amidst an archipelago of islands not laid down in any chart; indeed I was given to understand that the coast from Cape Providence to Cape Victory is but very imperfectly laid down by preceding navigators: these rocks bore to the east, S.E. by S. and to the west S.S.W. On the 22d we again weighed, the wind blowing fresh; at about thirty minutes past nine we saw the Evangelists, and as it now blew much fresher, we bore up for Separation Harbour. On the 24th and 25th we were off the Evangelists, the centre of them bearing W. ½ S. and on the 24th the captain went on shore at Cape Victory to fix its latitude. The weather at this time was particularly fine and pleasant, not a cloud was to be seen, "Ocean slumbered like an unweaned child," and harmony and good-fellowship reigned among us. We had met with no savages since leaving Separation Harbour, nor could any traces of their huts or wigwams be found on the land about Cape Victory, or in any of the coves or bays where we touched; we therefore concluded that this part of the coast is but little frequented by the natives.

As we were now upon our return, I shall speak briefly as possible of the different lagoons, coves, and harbours we met with, for I apprehend that a full description of them would be tiresome to the general reader; and I have avoided, for the same reason, an account of the different depths of water, and the rise and fall of the tide, and all geographical descriptions, as there are some well-penned relations by the preceding navigators upon that head, and I have therefore considered any notice from me upon these matters altogether unnecessary; and if in this narrative I should be found to differ from others in any former account of the Patagonians and Terro del Fuégians, it will be remembered that, "I speak not to disprove what Brutus spoke, but here I am to speak what I do know."

On the 27th we weighed from Port Tuesday on our return: standing over to the northern shore, we brought up in an immense bay, where there is a good anchorage, and called by the captain, Cape Parker. It is an open roadstead, having three low flat islands at each side athwart its mouth. The northern side of this bay is very shallow to a great extent; and the interior of the country partakes of the usual desolation, swampy grounds, cataracts, and large ponds of water.

This bay seems to have escaped the notice of all the preceding navigators, as it is not laid down in any chart of the coast. Captain Stokes and Lieutenant Skyring were engaged the whole afternoon, mid-deep in water, in making a survey of the northern part of the anchorage; and notwithstanding the weather was cold and rainy, they pursued their observations with unremitting activity and perseverance. While Captain Stokes was thus engaged, Lieutenant Sholl and myself rounded a sandy beach at this part of the bay; on proceeding onwards we heard a roaring of water, and on breaking our way through the forest, we came to a large cataract rolling its foaming course over a steep bank, above which the country appeared to be divested of wood. Having with some difficulty crossed this torrent, we came to an open plain, about two hundred paces in breadth and half a mile in length; on either side of this treeless space the mountains rose to a great altitude, thickly wooded with trees of all sizes, some withered and bleached by age, others of a green and lively verdure. A deadly silence reigned in this solitude, if we except the now fainter sounds of the waterfall, whose distant murmurings served but to heighten the effect of the surrounding desolation. As we walked along, we came to a natural pond of about thirty yards in circumference. I tasted the water and found it very sweet and good. On regaining the beach, we discovered among some bushes a quantity of muscle and limpet shells, and a few steps further in the forest we came upon a regular *kraal*, or village of deserted wigwams of various sizes. The natives must have remained here some time, for on all sides of these skeleton huts were strewed a great number of well-picked bones, we supposed of the seal and otter, although some of them appeared like the thigh-bone of a child. We searched all the wigwams in hope of meeting with some shells, but all these drinking cups had been removed. There must have been rare feasting at this place; and I strongly suspected them to be cannibals and a little wolfish in their appetite, from an incident which occurred in the wigwam of Old Cheop at Separation Harbour. I had one morning paid a visit to the wigwam, and being seated inside I had taken off my jacket for the younger Indian to admire, and having my shirt sleeve above my elbow, I proceeded to search round the hut for some spear heads, when Old Cheop suddenly clutched me by the elbow with one hand, while with the other he clawed and rubbed my naked arm. Whether he was struck by the difference of complexion from his own brown pelt, or fancied a broil (there was a good fire at the time in the wigwam), I know not; but certain it was that he talked to the younger savage very earnestly, who also seized my arm and held it very tight, at the same time he exchanged, I conceived, an anthropophagic look with the capacious mouthed Cheop. At this time the younger Indian let go his hold and stirred up the fire, both of them making low moaning and clucking noises (as if they had got the "rattles" in their throat) for some minutes. During this strange exhibition of civilities I sat very quiet; but I unhesitatingly declare, that had I met with these natives in any of my sporting excursions away from the ship, this sort of behaviour would have made me very uneasy, and have been quite a sufficient inducement for me to have left their company without a moment's delay. Captain Stokes had taken the cutter round a point farther to the northward, whence, after a considerable delay, she returned, and we rejoined the Beagle.

Captain Stokes having made a particular survey of this place, we weighed and came to an anchor in a bay under Cape Tamur, perhaps as bad an anchorage as any in the straits, being a very open roadstead. The difficulty is in getting close under the cape, in consequence of the many rocks, and the wind blowing directly from the west.

On the 1st of March we came-to in a bay under Cape Upright, where there is a good anchorage. We cruised in the gig round the harbour, which is of great extent, and goes some distance inland; it would prove an excellent and secure rendezvous for small vessels. We saw several birds in this anchorage considerably larger than a goose; their wings are very short, so as not to admit of their rising out of the water; but when disturbed, they move along the surface with great swiftness, beating the sea with their wings, and from the noise and rapidity of motion, we gave them the name of "steamers." There are some birch and pine trees in this harbour in good condition, and also the winter bark.

On March 3d, got under way, and at 4 P. M. made Cape Monday, bearing W. N. W. and Cape Notch, E. by N.; the weather became squally, upon which we bore up and run towards a harbour. At five, we were surprised at seeing a boat in a S. E. direction, apparently making towards us; fired four signal guns that she might not mistake our position, as we were now getting close in-shore. About half-past six she came alongside, and proved to be a whale-boat, with six men in her, belonging to a schooner, (the Prince of Saxe Cobourg,) Captain Brisbane, that had been wrecked on the 19th of December, in Fury Harbour, at the south entrance of the Barbara Channel. These men had been dispatched by Captain Brisbane towards the western entrance, in the hope of falling in with a South-Sea whaler, and it proved a lucky circumstance to them that they chanced to meet with the Beagle, as no vessel had hove in sight during our stay in that latitude. They represented the situation of Captain Brisbane as extremely perilous, the Fuegians becoming daily more numerous, and displaying hostile inclinations. The natives, when but few in number, are civil enough, and you may strip and leave them bare with impunity; but I do not consider it at all safe to fall in with them when they have a manifest advantage, as you may get knocked on the head for the sake of a string of beads or a few buttons, although, in some instances, the crew of the whale-boat had met with particular kind treatment from some of the families and tribes at the different lagoons wherein they sheltered for the night, for they soon made up a fire, assisted in drawing up the boat, and brought them plenty of fish, limpets, and muscles; but this was not always the case, for meeting one day with a number of large canoes full of these savages, they instantly gave chace to the whale-boat, shooting after them with their bows and arrows, and throwing their spears, and, with some difficulty, she escaped by the quickness and superiority of her pulling.

Captain Stokes consequently lost no time in proceeding to Port Gallant, in which we were moored on the 4th instant, and found that since our departure from this harbour the natives had paid it a visit, and had erected several wigwams; they had, however, quitted the place, and had taken with them the boarding-pikes which we had left standing on the beach. The next day, Lieutenant Sholl was dispatched in the whale-boat to Port Famine, with four men, victualled for twenty-one days, with dispatches for Captain King, to prevent any uneasiness which might arise in consequence of remaining absent from the Adventure for a much longer period than had been calculated upon. The same day Captain Stokes, the master, and Mr. Kirke, midshipman, with the six shipwrecked seamen and some of our own crew, proceeded in the launch and cutter to the relief of Captain Brisbane, at Fury Harbour, about seventy miles distant from Port Gallant. They returned on the 8th, bringing away Captain Brisbane and the rest of the shipwrecked seamen. Mr. Kirke related to me a few particulars of their passage. About midway in the Barbara Channel, they encountered a great many Indians in their canoes, who endeavoured to keep up with the launch and cutter, and as the boats neared any of the natives occupying the rocks and headlands (which in a great many places were thronged by them), they, as the boats passed underneath, set up a halloo, and discharged their arrows and spears, which, however, fell greatly short of the mark; but how great was the surprise of Captain Stokes and the rest of the officers, to behold some of these naked savages running along the beach, holding in their hands the identical boarding-pikes which had been missed from Port Gallant on our return. These pikes they flourished over their heads in a formidable manner, and this conduct made the captain still more anxious to make all haste to the relief of Captain Brisbane. Our party were happy to find, on their arrival at Fury Harbour, all of them in perfect safety, although they had been terribly alarmed by the report of one of their men, who was stationed on an adjacent mountain upon the look-out for the return of the whale-boat. This man, perceiving two large boats at a distance pulling towards Fury Harbour, was seized with a panic, and running down the mountain, he rushed into the tent, erected by Captain Brisbane, crying out, "The Indians! the Indians!" In an instant they all armed themselves, in the idea that the Indians were attacking them *en masse;* and what made this supposition the more probable, was their conduct a day or two previous, when they made an attack upon the stores, thieving every thing they could lay their hands on, and were only prevented entering the tent by the determined resistance of Captain Brisbane and his crew. As they had departed suddenly, Captain Brisbane conjectured they might return in greater numbers, and expecting an attack, he had made preparations for blowing them up with gunpowder, having placed three or four small barrels near their usual landing-place. Our party found on their arrival the place in a good state of defence, and had the Indians commenced hostilities, they would not have had much the best of the fight; however, the shipwrecked party were agreeably surprised on discovering their mistake, and manifested the greatest joy at their unexpected deliverance.

As the party were returning, they landed where a great many Indians had collected, most of whom were painted or daubed over the face and body, red and white, and such was the miserable state of some of these tribes, that they hardly appeared the figures of men; however, they were very friendly, and a good many lances and bows and arrows were obtained from them, in exchange for beads, knives, &c.; also two of their dogs, which are a breed resembling a fox, all but in colour, which is of a dirty grey cast; the head is sharp, ears long, and the tail bushy. Belonging to our ship's crew there was a black man, who had gone in the cutter, and he no sooner landed among the natives than they all gathered round him, astonished at his black face, and uttering strange sounds, pointed at him with their fingers, and kept touching his face and pulling his woolly head, laughing loudly, and indulging in many extravagant gestures, as if delighted at his sable appearance; nor could they believe for some time that it was his real colour; when, however, they became satisfied of this fact, their joy was unbounded, and they began to dab him with a sort of red earth, which they carried with them in a seal-skin bag. But "blackey" not relishing the metamorphose, he broke through the swarm which encircled him, and made for the boat, into which he jumped, concealing himself from view at the bottom of it; nor could he be persuaded to venture among them again, although they followed him to the boat, and beckoned him to come on shore, holding out their bows and arrows as an inducement; but it was all to no purpose, so they amused themselves by pointing and laughing at his woolly head whenever he raised it above the sides of the boat.

We left Port Gallant on the 10th, and the same day joined the Adventure in Port Famine, having been absent from her fifty-four days. At our approach she manned her yards and gave us three cheers. It is needless to express the joy manifested on our return—

> "The smile, the question, and the quick reply,
> And the heart's promise of festivity,"—

for our lengthened absence from the ship had created in Captain King and all his officers a most painful anxiety.

The Adventure had been newly painted, and looked exceedingly gay, and the Beagle also was smart enough when she first sailed out of Port Famine;

"How like the prodigal doth she return with overweathered ribs, and ragged sails, lean, rent, and beggared by the strumpet wind."—*Merchant of Venice.*

All on board the Adventure remarked an alteration in our personal appearance, and I believe none of us looked much the fatter for our excursion; we were, however, glad to see them looking so well, and their society and a little good cheer soon made us forget the fatigues and difficulties we had undergone.

During our absence, they had manned two boats, in which the master, second mate, a midshipman, and clerk, had proceeded to the opposite side of the strait, facing Port Famine, upon a shooting excursion, and having remained there a day or two, had arrived nearly mid-channel on their return back, when they were overtaken by one of those severe squalls so prevalent in these straits; and from the tempestuous weather which had now set in, accompanied by a heavy tumbling sea, it required the greatest caution to prevent their being swamped. One of the boats had shot a considerable distance a-head when, on looking back, they perceived the cutter keel uppermost, and their unfortunate companions struggling with the waves; they quickly bore down to their assistance, and the cutter having righted, they saw Mr. Ainsworth (the master) and Mr. Hodgskin (the clerk) succeed in getting into her, when she was again upset, and they had to renew the struggle for their lives. The other boat neared them fast, and Mr. Ainsworth and Mr. Hodgskin and the crew were observed clinging to the sides of the cutter, almost exhausted. Mr. Williams (second mate) hallooed to encourage them still to hold on; in a minute afterwards they were alongside—but too late. Poor Ainsworth had finally sunk, but not before he had saved the life of Mr. Hodgskin, who having lost his hold, exclaimed, "Oh, Ainsworth, save me!" when the noble fellow at once reached to him one hand, holding on with the other; his sinking companion seized it, and was thereby enabled to regain his hold of the cutter. A few minutes afterwards, poor Ainsworth suddenly disappeared, being unable longer to sustain the weight of his heavy boots and flushing dress, in the pockets of which were several pounds of shot. Mr. Hodgskin was dragged into the other boat, more dead than alive. Three of the men were also drowned, but had it not been for the skill and coolness displayed by Mr. Wilson (midshipman) and Mr. Williams, the whole party would inevitably have met a similar fate. After this lamentable disaster, the survivors thought it most advisable to bear up for the nearest point of land, and running in-shore, landed in a cove, where they passed the night. Early the next morning they set sail and arrived on board the Adventure.

Poor Ainsworth! his good companionable qualities had endeared him to his brother officers, and his loss was much regretted; soon afterwards, Captain King caused a memento of this unhappy event to be erected on a conspicuous part of Port Famine.

This place on our first arrival abounded in snipe, two or three brace flying up every ten paces, but the surgeon of the Adventure (a most excellent shot) had made such havoc among them, that they were soon much thinned; I therefore extended my researches alongshore for some miles, bivouacking in the gipsy style; and not wanting materials for making a fire, a teal or a wild duck often made an excellent repast. One day being out,—and as I always preferred wandering from the beaten track, and rambling towards a part of the coast perhaps never before visited by human being,—I found myself about two o'clock in the afternoon some three or four leagues from the ship, and being fatigued with so long a walk I stopped in a small cove, where I made a fire, and whilst busily employed in roasting a teal, I was surprised to hear the sharp bark of a dog at no great distance from me. Alarmed at the noise I started up, and seizing my gun, ran towards the sea-shore, expecting to see a tribe of Fuegians close upon me; but I was somewhat relieved by seeing only one Indian about one hundred paces from me; he came running quickly over the broken rocks towards the place where I stood, alarmed, no doubt, by the dog, and making his way to ascertain the cause of its barking. At the sight of me he stopped and crouched down, but in a moment afterwards darted into the woods, which skirt the beach for miles alongshore, followed by his fourfooted companion. He had been, by his appearance, upon a hunting excursion, for he was armed with a lance, and was doubtless a good way from his wigwam. By the suddenness of his departure, I was prevented from asking him to dinner; however, I walked to the place where he had disappeared, and waited some time in the hope of seeing him again, but by his not making his appearance, I concluded he had made the best of his way back through the woods to his tribe, and I returned also to my fireside, where I found the teal, for want of proper attendance, rather scorched; but I sat down with a good appetite, occasionally glancing among the bushes expecting to see an Indian staring at me from amidst the thickets by which I was surrounded. On again visiting this spot about three weeks afterwards, I found two or three wigwams had been erected near it in the interim.

The Adventure yawl had returned from a survey of the coast about Port Valdez, and they had met with several families of natives, and found them very friendly, and not of that marauding character which Captain Brisbane had observed of those in the Barbara Channel. The greater part of the Beagle's crew were now on shore towards the S. W. end of the bay, employed in washing their clothes, &c., and one afternoon, Mr. Bynoe and myself having been out shooting in that direction, we were surprised to find a number of the men employed hauling on a rope fixed to the top of a large tree, whilst others were engaged in setting it on fire and digging round the root. Upon inquiry of one of the seamen (Waller) who was amusing himself at a tub, washing his clothes, with a pipe in his mouth, as to what occasioned all this noise and bustle, he said that he had seen an immense black snake go under the root of the tree: but there was something in the dry manner in which he said this, that convinced us he was enjoying what he would have called *a lark;* however, it being no business of ours, we waited to see the event. Soon afterwards, Lieutenant Sholl, who had the care of the men on shore, and who was heading the party, came up to us, and said, "I dare say, when I get this snake that I shall be obliged to give it up as a specimen:" upon which we remarked, that possibly he might elude that claim; and he was about to reply, when one of the sailors cried out, "Mind, my boys, here he is—I hear him hiss," when Lieutenant Sholl ran towards them, exclaiming, "Take care he dont bite any of you, for it is certain death in a few moments." And now all was hurry and confusion, and hatchets and pikes were instantly upraised to knock the venomous reptile on the head the moment it appeared—for the tree had caught fire, and it was pulled up by the roots, the sailors giving a loud huzza as it fell to the ground with a great crash, blazing away most fiercely. Waller, during this uproar, continued at the tub, puffing out large streams of tobacco-smoke, and laughing away, in which we could not help joining. In the mean time the sailors busied themselves in searching for the snake, and Waller was questioned as to the size and length of it, and to the certainty of that being the tree; all of which questions he answered with great seeming confidence. Lieutenant Sholl loudly regretted its disappearance, and ordered the men to give up the search. Waller confessed to us, sometime afterwards, what we had all along suspected, that he had seen no snake, but that he had said so purposely to have some fun with his shipmates, not suspecting, at the time, that Lieutenant Sholl would interfere; but seeing him take so much interest in the affair, he was fearful of undeceiving him, lest he should be punished. We kept the secret accordingly. During our stay at Port Famine we were not visited by the natives, although on the opposite side of the strait the smoke of large fires was visible. One afternoon, Mr. Flinn and Dr. Bowen went over to meet the inhabitants, and succeeded in obtaining from some of the native women a few wicker baskets and spear heads. Whether these gentlemen had, like Dr. Pangloss (as observed by Miss Cunegund) been giving lessons in experimental philosophy, I cannot possibly determine, but they returned with their clothes confoundedly be-daubed with red paint.

Mr. Anderson, the botanist, was particularly indefatigable at this harbour, and generally returned from his excursions with some singular specimens of birds and flowers. I had extended my walk one morning to a considerable distance from the ship, and shot several parroquets, when I was surprised to hear loud hammerings proceeding from various parts of the wood in which I was, and shortly a flock of birds (larger than a thrush) flew past me with loud cries, and settled on the different trees around; they commenced hammering with great force with their long beaks against the bark, producing a noise like people at work upon a boat. The plumage of these birds is extremely beautiful. On the back of the neck and head, which are of a bright red colour, is a long tuft of red feathers, which was finely erected as they darted up the trees; I soon put a stop to the loud peckings of some, and being anxious to possess as many of these birds as I could, I shot several, eagerly following in whatever direction they flew. I persevered then so far that, on thinking about returning, I found myself so bewildered in the intricacies of the forest, that I knew not which way to take for the sea shore. I walked one way, then another, but the farther I went the more I was puzzled. I then took to climbing one of the highest trees, in the hope of catching a glimpse of the sea, but nothing appeared save the leafy forest around me, and I descended, cursing the red-headed woodpeckers and my own precipitate stupidity in losing myself. After endeavouring unsuccessfully for more than an hour to find my way back, I began to experience some very unpleasing reflections, and sat down beside a small uprooted tree to deliberate, or rather to soliloquise; but I soon bethought myself that remaining at the root of a tree in useless reflection would utterly fail in extricating me from the difficulty. I therefore plucked up courage and again floundered on, exercising my swearing talents with great eloquence to keep my spirits up, and at length came to a small rivulet which ran meandering through the woods; and recollecting that I had stepped over a small brook on first entering the forest, I followed the course of this stream, which fortunately for me pursued its course to the sea shore, and in about half an hour brought me (to my no small satisfaction) at the very spot where I entered the wood.

The time drew nigh, when a dinner was to be given on shore by Captains King and Stokes, to the officers of the expedition, and the tables which had been erected in the largest tent groaned under a profusion of roast and boiled, and other tender and savory meats, and of an infinite number of wild fowl, together with vast quanties of tongues and hams, and also some tureens, which put some of us in rapture when we knew these to contain mock turtle soup, made from an old pig which had been on board some time, and had had the range of Port Famine for a long period. This rich soup, with a plenty of puddings and pies, formed our repast. The wines also were rich and good; and a number of decanters of port and sherry, Teneriffe and Madeira, were distributed about the table. It was not in the nature of some in our berth to view these preparations without feeling an eager anxiety (which we concealed as well as we could) to commence operations; and by the time the dinner hour had arrived, we were in excellent spirits to do justice to so ample a display. Captain King was the president, on the right hand of whom sat Captain Stokes, and on the left Mr. Atrill (whose affections seemed entirely captivated by the tureens, which he surveyed with evident pleasure). Lieutenant Sholl officiated as vice-president; and now the soup-ladles were never still, and Captain King was sufficiently employed in distributing it quick enough. Mr. Atrill pronounced it to be "excellent soup," and he came in for a good share of the forced meat balls, while the rich grease ran down the sides of his mouth and glistened upon his chin. Every person seemed to enjoy the dinner, and the various dishes were not long without customers: as for me, I was ashamed of eating so much, but looking round and seeing all as busily engaged as myself, I no doubt escaped observation. After the cloth was removed the wine circulated pretty freely, and the healths of many distinguished characters were drunk. Several songs were sung, and the greatest conviviality prevailed, and on the health of Captain King being proposed, that gentleman returned thanks in a neat and elegant speech, as did, likewise, Captain Stokes upon a like occasion. But nothing could equal the good-humour of our vice-president, who harangued the company with considerable talent, and by his own peculiar hilarity contributed much to the good fellowship of the evening; and in the plenitude of his joy he did not forget to eulogize the charms of young Maria, the *belle* of the Patagonians, and all of us wished once more to have a look at her Indian phiz. I could perceive that more than one of the gentlemen gave evident signs of being *Bacchi plenus,* and the purser by this time had some difficulty in preserving his equilibrium. Captain King (who had been conversing with Captain Stokes) now turned round to make some observation to Mr. Atrill, but the purser, not waiting to hear what he had to say, suddenly fell backwards off the form, giving the table a kick with his feet as he fell. Being quickly raised up by some persons in attendance, he resumed his seat, saying " he thought there had been backs to them:" it was all to no purpose; two minutes afterwards he fell over in the same manner, and was dragged out underneath the tent. The clerk, who had observed him vanish so unceremoniously, staggered out to look after him, and the purser perceiving him said, " won't you support the button?" upon which the clerk caught hold of Mr. Atrill to keep him up, but unfortunately he somehow or another rolled into a ditch, dragging the purser in after him. The clerk, on getting out, was heard to say, " I'm not drunk," but it was said a great many believed otherwise at the time. The vice-president, who had often during the evening " set the table in a roar," was now seen quietly to slide off his seat, and crawl away upon his hands and knees. Captains King and Stokes soon after leaving the table, we broke up, and I went to Mr. Harrison's tent, where I thought I had secured a berth; but I found it occupied, whereupon I enveloped myself in a large cloak, and lay down in one corner. About four in the morning we were all woke up by the vice-president, who on leaving the table had fallen asleep among the bushes, and he had just awoke, almost frozen, it being "a nipping and an eager air;" but on looking round the tent what was our surprise to see extended a tall figure in uniform, with a blanket rolled tightly round his head. Upon disturbing him, he turned out to be the assistant-surgeon of the Adventure, who was at a loss to know in what latitude he was, not recollecting when he came into the tent.

On the 7th of April we departed from Port Famine, and in the evening came-to in Fresh Water Bay. On the 8th we brought up in a bay near Cape Negro, the western point of Elizabeth Island, bearing N. N. W., and Quarter-Master's Island N. E. ½ E. On the morning of the 10th we again saw the smoke arising from the fires of the Patagonians, and as we neared Gregory Bay, we could perceive the coast lined with them; some were standing on horses' backs, and waving large skins to and fro in the air, past six o'clock we came-to at this anchorage, and one of the boats being manned, Lieutenant Sholl and Dr. Bowen went on shore. The doctor returned about two in the morning, bringing with him three of the Patagonians, Lieutenant Sholl remaining behind as a hostage for their safe return. In the morning, Mr. Atrill endeavoured to obtain one of the curiously-painted skins in which they were wrapped, by offers of beads and knives; but these proving an inadequate temptation, Mr. A. brought from below an old sword, and striding about the deck, he flourished it over his head several times. The idea of possessing this formidable, and to them novel weapon, acted like enchantment. One of them more active than the rest immediately threw his skin to Mr. Atrill, and snatched away the sword. On going ashore soon afterwards, I remarked this Indian walking from the beach towards his companions with an air of great grandeur, with head erect, and displaying vast importance, before an old Indian. The cacique (for such he proved to be) no sooner beheld the sword, than, running to the possessor, he had it the blade from the scabbard, waving it in the air, and returning it, afforded him great delight. These manœuvres he practised ten or a dozen times, laughing each time he drew and viewed the glittering blade. Sometimes he would draw the sword and make a cut with it, straightening his arm close to his side, in the manner represented in the drawing, and this position he would keep for some time.

The beach was now for a considerable distance thronged by the natives, and there might have been collected in men, women, and children, from three to four hundred people. They were evidently assembled for the purpose of barter, for an innumerable quantity of ostrich feathers (of no value), skins of the guanacoe, and other animals, were laid out upon the stubble, as if for inspection. Almost all the Indians were on horseback, and a number of large dogs were to be seen crouching down among those who had dismounted and arranged themselves in different groups; altogether they must have possessed nearly 150 dogs, and some of these animals (in packs of twenty or thirty together) were observed ranging the plain in various directions. Such an assemblage of savage-looking people, of all ages, even children at the breast, intermingled with horses and dogs, was altogether a novel sight, particularly when parties of them were squatting in circles round large fires cooking horseflesh. A great many of them were young, and rather handsome for Indians; while others were old, and as frightful as it is possible to conceive anything in human shape to be. Some wore a single ostrich feather on one side of the head, kept on by a string of hide tied over it. The men were not muscular, their legs and arms having a roundness and appearance entirely feminine. Meeting with Lieutenant Sholl, I asked him how he had passed the night among them; he told me that they made him up a bed of skins, and ranged themselves all round him, when he fell fast asleep, nor did they awaken him until the morning, he having slept as well as ever he did in his life. Upon my inquiring after "Young Maria" (for I had not met with her), he began to laugh heartily; and on asking the occasion of his mirth, I was not a little surprised to hear that "Maria" had turned out to be a *gentleman*; this discovery caused much mirth amongst us, but as all were equally deceived, the features and expression being decidedly feminine, the shaft of ridicule was blunted against any one in particular.

As I understood their encampment to be distant about five miles from the sea shore, I proceeded in the direction pointed out to me by an officer of the Adventure who had visited it, and giving the rein to the horse, I was carried at a swift canter over a level country, which was, as far as I could see on all sides, deeply indented by the horses' hoofs, proving that the Patagonians had been in the neighbourhood a considerable time. Having ridden about four miles, I perceived, in a gentle declivity, towards which I was fast approaching, a smoke arising from a large fire, burning briskly; around it were huddled a number of young Patagonian females,

> "A' plump and strapping in their teens,"

apparently busied in cooking some kind of flesh. On my riding up, some withdrew from the fire and came towards me, with merry and laughing faces, making signs for me to dismount and sit down among them. Not being averse to merry society, I did not hesitate to accept their courteous offer; and, tying my horse to a piece of stubble, I seated myself amidst these tawny and almost naked savages. The eldest did not appear more than twenty-five years of age, and might have been considered well looking, but for her long ragged hair, streaming down over her shoulders and as low as her waist; this however gave to her face a singular wildness of expression, heightened by her black and piercing eyes, which were painted underneath with red and black patches. They offered me a portion of the meat they were preparing, a proof of their hospitality, with which I would readily have dispensed, but not thinking it courteous to refuse, I chewed a piece for some time, until disgust overcoming my politeness, I suddenly ejected the nauseous and bitter food with a spattering noise, to their evident confusion and amazement. At this breach of good manners, the elder looked very displeased, and immediately gnawed off another piece, which she thrust into my hand, exclaiming, *cavallo*, (the Spanish for horse); this expression was repeated by the rest of the group, and they all endeavoured to convince me how good it was, by eating voraciously of it themselves. Thus was my good-nature most severely taxed, but wishing to be friendly rather than otherwise, I constrained myself to gorge a considerable quantity, which, in a short time, produced very uncomfortable sensations, and notwithstanding they said it was *cavallo*, I strongly suspected it to be the flesh of some other animal, from its being so exceedingly strong and bitter. During our repast, I observed many of them talking together of me and laughing, while those nearest me were continually inserting their hands in my hair, and pulling open my waistcoat. One of the *young ladies* came and sat down by my side, and after looking steadily in my face, she also began to unbutton my waistcoat, and talked and laughed to the others. Not much admiring these extravagances, as they got rather noisy and beset me too closely to be agreeable, (for they forcibly took out of my pockets most of the tobacco and beads that happened to be there), I began to fear that, being a good way from my companions, they might also take a fancy to my jacket and trousers; I therefore threw some buttons to a distance from me, and they no sooner ran to pick them up, than I disengaged the horse's reins from the stubble, and leaped upou his back, applying the sharp spurs to his sides. The Indians no sooner perceived me galloping away, than they commenced a loud and wild halloo, such as we may suppose was set up after Tam O'Shanter,

"When out the hellish legion sallied."

I pursued my way towards the camp, perceptible a good distance a-head, and in a short time I arrived at these habitations, which consisted of about fifteen or twenty huts, formed of poles and skins, and built in the same manner as our gingerbread booths at a fair, enclosed on three sides, and entirely open in front; between each hut there was a space of three or four yards. Having tied the horse to the poles of the first, I walked in, and beheld seated in one corner a Patagonian woman, who was rolling up compositions of earth, of various colours, red, black, and white; these she formed to about the size and length of a stick of sealing-wax, and were used for beautifying themselves in the manner previously described. She was exceedingly good-tempered, and kept laughing to another woman, who was squatted down just outside the hut, and they both frequently looked at me very significantly, repeating the words *chick, chick, chick*. The sides of the hut were hung round with strange implements of their manufacture; and what appeared worthy of notice were the *ballas*, of a much superior size and make to those I had seen round the waists of the Patagonians on the beach; I therefore purchased two or three pairs for some beads and tobacco. On going to the other huts, I found them entirely vacated, these two women and an old Indian being the only persons now left in the encampment. On the outside of the dwellings were hung several heads and shoulders of deer, which apparently had not been long killed;

these were secured for the benefit of the mess. There were a great many dogs prowling about the place, but they took no notice.

The following is a description of one of their tombs which I visited. In the centre of a circular trench, of about a foot in depth, and twelve or fourteen yards in circumference, a number of bushes and skins were raised up in the form of a cone, to the height of twelve or fifteen feet; the top of the cone was closely covered in with bushes and skins, and surmounted by two small red flags; around the outside of the trench were placed, at certain distances, several flags of a similar description. But what had the most singular appearance, were the effigies of two horses, made out of skins, which were placed, the nose of one of them resting on a stick, close outside the trench. As I was viewing this tomb, an old Indian approached me in great grief, making a loud and doleful outcry, with a singular variation of note, which he continued as long as I remained near the place.

On my return to the encampment, many of the

natives had arrived from the beach, some of whom did not seem best pleased at my having possessed myself of their property; they pointed to several of their implements which I had fastened around me, muttering to each other; but as I had obtained them in fair exchange from the old Indian and the two women, who would not only have sold all the moveables that were in the huts, but the huts likewise, so soliciteous were they to possess the beads, buttons, and tobacco, I did not feel disposed to relinquish them. One of the women,

"A souple jade she was and strang."

now rushed forward, and seizing me by the girdle, dragged me along with great ease, and endeavoured to deprive me of the *ballas*. Not much fancying the grasp of this giantess, I made violent efforts to disengage myself, but she did not let go her hold until she had made me relinquish one set of the *ballas*. After my release I was not long in mounting my horse, and riding off as fast as I could. On my arrival at the beach I perceived a crowd of Patagonians engaged in what I imagined to be a religious ceremony; they were assembled round an elderly woman, who held in her hands a small wooden *christo* (so she called it), at the sight of which the people set up a loud howl; then descending into a lone tone of voice, they uttered many dismal groans; these again broke out into discordant kind of singing, all the while smearing themselves with red and white paint, spitting in the palms of their hands, and slapping themselves over the face, arms, and legs. Altogether it was a strangely wild scene. Is there not a possibility of reclaiming them from these absurdities? and there would be an original glory (left, no doubt, for some of our missionaries), in making these people desist from practising such fooleries around little *Christo*, and the hallelujahs of the Patagonians would be finer to hear "than all the bells in Christendom."

Since these people have been known, they do not seem to have altered: wrapped in the guanacoe skin, and inured from infancy to privation, they range the desert uncontrolled; subservient to no law or will but their own, they undoubtedly possess a contentment and a delight in their native wilds inconceivable to the inhabitants of the civilised world.

I was again surrounded by several of the party, who recognising the articles I had brought from their camp, an old cacique rode up to me, holding up his hands, and, with great emphasis, pronounced the words *malo, malo!* then pointing with his finger in the direction of the encampment, said, *ahi, ahi!* and motioned to the others to take them away; but I managed to get off, and gave them in charge to one of the sailors who had the care of the boat. I compromised with them afterwards, for some strings of beads and knives, and they were well satisfied. Among these people were found a bow and quiver of arrows of a similar description to those used by the natives of Terra del Fuégo, and an Indian was pointed out as a native of that island; he was of short stature, but I could not recognise any other distinction, he being habited like a Patagonian; he appeared to be one of them, and was no doubt perfectly reconciled to his fate: he certainly had joined a better mess, but how he came among them is another affair, and of which we could give no account. Being seated on a bank with one of the Indians, I showed him a picture of old Che-re-cow-wow, which I had brought with me on shore, and at the same instant I pointed to the land of Terra del Fuégo, which is plainly to be seen from Gregory bay. He looked at the savage, and, laughing, pointed over to the land likewise, and exclaimed, *Zapoliens!*—the name, I supposed, given by the Patagonians to the Fuegian Indians. Dr. Bowen, whilst engaged talking to the cacique, chanced to tread upon one of the dogs, when the animal immediately flew at him, and was instantly aided and abetted by some others, and the entire pack would soon have followed, had not some of the Indians arose simultaneously and beaten them off.

About three o'clock in the afternoon the bay presented a very animated appearance; it seemed as if others of the Patagonians, who in the early part of the day were straggling about the wild recesses of this part of the country, had arrived at their camp, and being apprised of our landing, they had now rode up to welcome and greet our arrival on their shores. Several fires were kindled on the beach in various places, and parties were to be seen busily engaged in cooking portions of venison and other flesh, while others were making preparations to do the same, having only to unloose a small string which confined large lumps of *cavallo* to their naked sides. On these occasions the most perfect amity appeared to subsist among them, and at their dinner hour, at any rate, they were not required to pay particular attention to their caciques, for a very broad, squat-faced Patagonian, who bore that appellation, possessed of a most capacious chest and brawny shoulders, thrust himself among the dingy circle, and having unflanked himself from a *cincture* of guanacoe flesh, he quickly conveyed it among the glowing embers, watching in seeming ecstasy the flaring morsel, until it had become as dark as his own black and ragged locks. They were all, and at the same time, equally busy about the fire, each turning and roasting his individual portion. The greater part, when the flesh was sufficiently blackened, withdrew it from the fire and sank their well-arranged teeth into it, gnawing, or rather tearing off, some good mouthfuls; but I observed many preferred having a feed *peu cuit*; but these were few in proportion to the others. It was easy to perceive their appetites were of the first order; and perhaps it is fortunate that nature has given them a very capacious swallow, for a roll and a turn appeared to be quite sufficient for mastication. I only noticed one instance of a slight mistake being made by one of the party, who, I suppose, had ventured upon too large a *fid*, for I could perceive him begin to stare like a throttled earwig; but after a few outstretchings of neck he bolted it very comfortably, and in a short time regained his composure. As this circumstance did not excite the notice of the party, I naturally concluded that such an occurrence was not at all unusual.

When the cacique had finished his dinner, he sought out, as he had hitherto done, Captain King, to whom he was constantly pointing out from among the assembled group the different caciques and their sons; and all of the sons, I must say, with only one exception, were stupid-looking "six-feet sucklings." The countenance of one of the caciques' sons evinced greater expression of mind, and he seemed to possess more activity than the rest, for he was seldom still, and kept looking eagerly round, as if to see that all was quiet, and that no row took place among his people and our party; at least, it struck me to be his endeavour to preserve order, for suddenly the bluff-headed cacique ran up to Captain King, crying out "capitan, capitan," and pointed with his finger to the beach, where a sailor was seen mounted on horseback, seemingly much against the will of one of the Patagonians, who was endeavouring to unhorse him, but Jack held on like a Briton, and away went the horse at a full gallop. Many of the Patagonians gave chase, no doubt to pull him off, but Jack was so malicious as to balk their intention, by suffering a somerset over the horse's head. When this was perceived by the cacique's son, I saw him ride up to those of his party who had given chase, and talk to them, and they all very speedily returned. Captain King also gave the sailor a slight intimation of what he might expect if he were again guilty of a like action.

I chanced to be upon the beach some short time afterwards, when I was joined by this son of a cacique, and also by the wheedling Indian, whom I formerly mentioned as having but one eye, when the former of them offered me rather a round stone, which was particularly smooth, and of a dark colour; as it did not appear to be of the least utility, I returned it to him. On my mentioning this circumstance on board (after we had left Patagonia), it was said that in all probability this might have been a bezoar stone, for which Sir John Narborough was indefatigable in searching the inside of the guanacoe. As I perceived the son of the cacique and him of the one eye walk towards a cluster of women, who were seated on a bank hard by, amusing themselves by chewing pigtail, I determined to accompany them, and therefore walked towards the group, and seated myself among them; but what was my surprise, when I was suddenly seized hold of by one of the party (it was a grasp I remembered very well), and on looking in her face I soon recognised her to be the lady who had so officiously dismantled me of the *ballas* at the encampment. She now made a great outcry of *pipa,* and thrusting her hand very unceremoniously into my waistcoat-pocket, pulled out a small Spanish pipe (a sort of Judy, about the size and length of what we see adorning the mouths of our sprat-women), which was no sooner in her possession than she filled it with tobacco, and running to a fire hard by, lighted her pipe, and returned in triumph to her seat upon the bank. I certainly had obtained, for some buttons, this identical tube of one of the women who saluted me with the cry of *chick, chick,* when I first saw them at the encampment, and on looking round I perceived the very individual herself stuck up among them. I very soon explained to the son of the cacique, by signs (which he understood very well), that I had given some buttons to Madame, who was laughing at me just opposite, and she had given the pipe in exchange; but I neither could recover one nor the other, notwithstanding he made every exertion to obtain possession, in which he was seconded by my one-eyed friend.

There was an old lady among the Patagonians who had two very pretty daughters, the eldest of whom was the handsomer, and she was a mother. The younger, to relieve her sister, I suppose, then cradled on her knee a staring infant, which looked like a little baboon with its head shaved; and as she acted in the capacity of chief nurse, she would frequently take the child in her arms, and holding its face before the dusky visage of the old woman, took great delight in observing that venerable lady fondle and talk to the child, which she did in such a strange manner, and made so many ugly and hideous faces, that I have no hesitation in saying that she would have frightened an English infant into fits. This young lady no sooner perceived that I noticed the child, than she beckoned me over to sit by her, an invitation I could not resist, and then she took great pains to convince me how clever she was, for having first unswathed the infant from several skins, she held up its little offensive frame for me to admire, and then proceeded (with repeated expectorations and other ablutions) in the usual duties of a nurse. After various scrapings and rubbings (which caused the little wretch to gape and throw out its legs and arms like an expiring frog), she wrapped it in some other skins, and after having conveyed it into a sort of cradle (resembling those in use among the Indians of North America), she slung the child at her back. I did all I could to appear gratified and pleased at the exhibition, and believe succeeded tolerably well; but not wishing another such infliction, I was about to take my departure, when I was prevented by the women, who did not wish me to leave them, and I therefore continued in gentle dalliance until an old Indian rode up to the group. As soon as he dismounted, I was seized with a desire to possess myself of the singular stirrups which dangled from the saddle, and I offered him such presents as I thought he would value, at the same time I intimated to him my wish of receiving the stirrups in exchange. He was proceeding to take them off to give them into my possession, when an old woman (his wife, I suppose,) rushed forward to prevent him, and attempted to divest him of the knives and tobacco I had given him; but this he resisted, and succeeded, notwithstanding her noisy interference, in placing the stirrups in my hands. This behaviour she was far from enduring with a tame submission, and she advanced towards him with her under-lip lowered down upon her chin (a very pretty and becoming method of showing her teeth and displeasure), when I placed, hoping to compound matters, a small looking-glass, and held it up that she might observe her own sweet countenance. The sight of her face (now rendered as ugly as possible by passion) instantly conveyed the highest gratification, and she surveyed herself with evident pleasure; and after a few innocent and playful curlings of nose, and twisting of lips, " for there was never yet fair woman but she made mouths in a glass," she appeared to be quite reconciled to the loss of the stirrrups, although she occasionally looked at them with a discontented eye; but when she observed me about to put them in my pocket, she broke out at the old Indian in a long, noisy jargon, and he now motioned me to go away, which I immediately did, leaving him to calm the angry dame, for she still continued talking in a very ill mood, which he good-humouredly listened to, and did not seem to heed.

> " It gars me greet
> To think how mony counsels sweet,
> How mony lengthen'd sage advices
> The husband frae the wife despises."

On my proceeding along the beach towards other crowds of them, I observed that a few were refreshing themselves with some ship biscuits, and occasionally putting a bottle to their mouths, which did not seem to hold water, but a liquor by far more palatable, and the tall old Indian (of whom I have made the drawing, and who was so fond of flourishing his sword) was engaged in busy conversation with Captain King, while other caciques were huddled round Captain Stokes, as if to ask

> " by what strange cause
> He sought these wilds, traversed by few?"

and they all appeared very desirous of being noticed by him. While I entertained myself in viewing the assembled tribe, and listening to the wild and unusual noises into which they sometimes broke out, I saw a young Indian approach who had purchased a sword and scabbard, but he found, on drawing the blade, that it was curtailed in the length by at least one-half. On perceiving this, he was evidently much vexed, and he went about showing the fragment of the blade to those around him, and seemed to be perfectly aware of the useless bargain he had made. But what added to his mortification was the old Patagonian, who now advanced, waving his long, shining sword, which he contrasted (his features assuming a smile of exultation) with the broken blade of the luckless Indian. My next care was to introduce myself among other parties of them (for I was always fond of variety), and, to my great amusement, I perceived a midshipman from the Adventure, sitting on a bank, in lively conversation with several handsome-looking Patagonian girls, who, perhaps, not understanding the smoothness of his face, succeeded in putting the young man to the blush, owing, very possibly, to the presence of some gentlemen from the Beagle, who had witnessed the amorous attack. As the evening set in, the Patagonian women were seen to load their horses with the numerous skins which had been spread out upon the shore, and mounting on the top, proceeded, with a slow pace, into the country; others still lingered on the beach, and to the very last seemed unwilling to part with us; some gratuitously offered their spurs and guanacoe skins, while many, more avaricious, were eager to make a good exchange. The Adventure's boat having shoved off for the ship, that of the Beagle soon followed, and as long as we remained in sight, many of the Patagonians, standing on their horses' backs, continued waving their guanacoe skins in token of farewel; but notwithstanding these marks of friendship and good-will, I could not help thinking, after my adventures among them, upon what Shylock observes to Bassanio.

"I will buy with you,
Sell with you, talk with you, walk with you,
And so following; but I will not eat with you,
Drink with you, nor pray with you."

The next morning the ships got under way, and soon passed the Narrows of the Hope. We again anchored in Possession Bay, and on looking towards the shore, we could perceive, but at a great distance inland, the smoke from the fires of other tribes of Patagonians, and from the quantity which spread over the face of the country, they might possibly have been nearly as numerous as those we had left at Gregory Bay. On looking towards the Fuegian coast, no smoke was now visible; and had it been requisite to have landed there when we first entered the straits and anchored in Possession Bay (for then an immense smoke was seen), although here, also, at a good distance inland, we doubtless should have encountered a formidable muster of the natives of Terra del Fuégo. The face of the country hereabouts is level, and we could not but observe the striking contrast between the western and the eastern entrance of the Straits of Magellan. The wind and weather being much in our favour, we very soon cleared the straits, and stood away for Monte Video. I believe that most in our berth were overjoyed at the prospect of replenishing our stock; for the greater part of our plates, dishes, and glasses, were broken, and all our spoons abridged in the handles; the teapot was without any handle at all, and had received some curious indentings, and the spout had got a slue to port. But what occasioned us to laugh, in spite of all these disasters, was the failure of an expedient to which the clerk had been reduced; for, not having a cabin, he had lashed up to the top of the berth, a quantity of the ship's papers, thinking they would ride in safety, but, one rough and unlucky day, at twelve o'clock, when we were all busily engaged in throwing down our *scaldings*, the lashings gave way, and the open list pitched out of the berth, the slop-book assaulted the red head of the steward, the allowance lists flew all over the table, and a flight of weekly accounts descended into the soup.

As I happened one day to be walking the deck with Captain Brisbane, the conversation turned upon Fury Harbour, and he related to me a *frâcas* which he had with the natives soon after he was wrecked; and while it substantiates, in some degree, what I have said about their *kindness* when they happen to have the superiority, it places beyond doubt their *friendly* intentions towards Captain Brisbane. One morning, shortly after the wreck, he was employed on board in saving what stores and provisions he could, when some canoes of Indians (as was their daily custom) came down upon him, and at first paddled round the ship, but soon afterwards they remained stationary almost close alongside, and appeared to be anxiously observing what was passing on board. As they had hitherto been tolerably harmless, and had interfered no further than by merely stealing various trifles which came in their way, he did not suspect them of any more sinister motive, when suddenly one of the canoes came close to the ship, while the other party paddled off to some distance, and there waited the return of the others. During this movement he observed that no women were in the canoes, but not suspecting from this circumstance that any mischief was intended, he pursued what he was about, and had just hooked up some clothing and other necessaries, when the party of Fuegians which had come alongside mounted the deck. As these savages take a great deal of notice, they soon commenced examining what was upon deck, and a coat and trousers became objects of much attention. Captain Brisbane had enough to do to make them throw down whatever they took up; but he might have spared himself that trouble, for when he succeeded in making them let go one thing, they had seized upon another. He soon found that he was much inconvenienced by their coming on board, and as they greatly disturbed him by giving utterance to a succession of clucking, unmeaning, and guttural sounds, he thought it best to give them some biscuits, which they gnawed with greedy and hungry appetites. As they now became more peaceable, he again busied himself about the wreck, and he had been but a few minutes engaged, when on looking round he perceived that his swarthy visitors were scrambling over the side in great haste, and that the trousers and other wearing apparel had vanished from the deck. On discovery of the theft, he was over the side in an instant, and was so fortunate, (or unfortunate if you will), as to jump into the canoe as they were about to push off, when they immediately seized their paddles and following the other canoes (which now darted away with exceeding swiftness towards the opposite shore) succeeded in conveying the captain off in triumph. It was therefore his first care, in this emergency, to give the nearest Indian a blow which tumbled him over the others to the further end of the canoe, and the rest, seeing him approach towards them with a marvellous fist, instantly set up a deplorable yell, and the canoe was almost immediately afterwards overturned. It was well for Captain Brisbane that he could swim like a duck, and being a man of great strength and activity, he quickly swam to the canoe (for the Indians had soon righted her) and was equally dexterous in getting in as soon as themselves, when they instantly upset her again; but this time he was the second who got in, and the others seemed to have had enough, for they made the best of their way towards the other canoes; and as they swam along, from their ragged streaming hair, and the wild savage noises they uttered, they might easily have been mistaken for so many sea monsters. The savage now in the canoe with Captain Brisbane, had began to paddle fast towards the shore, when the captain, seizing one of the oars, struck him a blow upon the arm which laid it open almost from the elbow to the shoulder. At this unavoidable salutation the savage set up a most infernal howl, but not heeding this loud outcry, Captain Brisbane motioned him to return to the ship, a sign which he perfectly understood, and set about immediately, as well as his wounded arm would allow him, and the captain assisted him with the paddle, which he sometimes flourished over his head to remind the Indian of what he might expect if he played off any Fuegian trick. In this manner they reached the vessel, when Captain Brisbane commenced a search for the clothing, but he could find only the trousers, which had been concealed under some skins at the bottom of the canoe. The native was suffered to depart without further molestation, and he paddled away, awkwardly enough, towards the migratory crew, who were seen waiting his arrival on the opposite shore.

The sailors who had been employed about the tent did not perceive the commencement of the fracas, but had now pushed off to the assistance of their commander, whom they joined on board the wreck. From some further conversation which I had respecting the country about Fury Harbour, I was led to believe that this part of Terra del Fuégo was intersected by various channels or rivers, which branching off in many directions, formed numerous islands, in which "no genial plant takes root, no verdure quickens," for all of them partake of that same desolation and rocky land which I have already said is met with from Port Gallant to Cape Pillar. I was also given to understand, that when Captain Weddell proceeded in the ship Jane, far to the southward of Cape Horn, that Captain Brisbane had the command of the Beaufoy in that expedition. Had we not been in company with the Adventure, we should have had a very quick run to the Rio de la Plata, but that ship sailed badly in light winds, and we were frequently obliged to shorten sail that we might not run a-head of her This delay proved vexing enough, but when we were about a hundred leagues from the river a dense fog set in, and although we strained our eyes to catch a sight of her, and burnt blue lights, and kept up a noisy thumping on the drum, yet it was of no avail; and considering that she was running fast for Monte Video, we lost no time in sailing after her, but by some means we arrived off that harbour a good many hours before she came in.

It was on the 24th of April, 1827, about one A. M., when the Beagle sailed into Monte Video roads, and as we were about to anchor we were hailed by a Brazilian man-of-war, who ordered us to bring-to, or she would fire into us; and as we kept running further into the harbour she fired an unshotted gun, and soon afterwards a musket ball whistled over our heads. We were speedily at quarters, for the whole harbour was in an uproar. The forts on shore began to fire signal guns, and blue lights blazed from most of the Brazilian men-of-war. Being now hailed by the Eclipse packet, we let go the anchor, and a boat soon afterwards came alongside, in which was the commander of the Liberal corvette (the Brazilian man-of-war which first hailed us), who stated to Captain Stokes that Admiral Brown, the Buenos Ayrian commander-in-chief, had recently given them battle in the River Plate, and that the Brazilians had lost in the engagement twelve vessels (which was not at all improbable, as they cannot fight), and that the Buenos Ayrian privateers came almost into the roads, which made them, as may be supposed, sufficiently on the alert. This explanation was deemed quite satisfactory, and the next morning we heard of the engagement in which Captain Shepheard, of the Perauga frigate, had been killed. This person was captain of the foretop on board this ship when she was commanded by Lord Cochrane.

Commodore Brown was badly wounded, and his first lieutenant (Drummond), after fighting the vessel in the most determined manner against several Brazilian schooners and brigs, was at last killed by an eighteen pound shot. I recollect seeing Drummond when he was imprisoned on board the Real Principe, in 1826, he was at that time in the Brazilian service, and had been a lieutenant on board of the Perauga frigate; but having incautiously betrayed his intention of joining the Buenos Ayrians, he had been seized, on his arrival at Rio Janeiro, and conveyed on board the prison ship, from which he made his escape, and eventually joined Commodore Brown. We found at this anchorage H. M. S. Ranger and the American corvette Boston, of twenty-two guns. We frequently met some officers from the latter ship at Rogers' Hotel. One of the midshipmen used to give, with great good humour, a specimen of the Yankee pronunciation of "O yes" and "O no;" and then remark upon the frequent application of the words "you know" among the English.

The houses at Monte Video are mostly flat-roofed, and when the weather happens to be fine and pleasant, those senhoras who are young and handsome, are sure to be seen walking on the house-top, enjoying the cool breezes, and directing the telescope towards most officers, who assemble likewise on the roof of the hotels. But when these fascinating senhoras perceive the telescopes directed towards themselves, the smile of unspeakable sweetness which illumines their countenance, and the look full of bewitching tenderness which they give you, prove how delighted they are in being noticed, and make you desirous of an immediate introduction to their society. Indeed, so fond are they of admiration that it is considered a great compliment to gaze at them some time; and so long as you continue, they will be sure to repay your attention by a profusion of smiles of approbation and encouragement. Even the old aya, or donna, will mount the stairs, dressed up for the occasion in silk attire, their heads adorned with roses, and appear desirous, by playing off a few amorous coquetries, to hold out upon a respectable footing. I noticed that Monte Video contained rather a greater sprinkling of unemployed gentlemen than when we left it; and the landing-place of a morning seemed to be the rendezvous of those who apparently had no visible means of living, and who appeared waiting for opportunities of proceeding to Buenos Ayres overland, a practice much in use, and in which they were greatly assisted by the guachos of the country.

Early in May, H.M.S. Ganges arrived at this harbour, and we were much rejoiced on receiving letters from home, and only those who have been on foreign stations can duly appreciate the pleasure of reading them. We remained at this pleasant anchorage for more than a fortnight, and everything being ready for our departure, we got under weigh for Rio Janeiro. But before I take my leave of Monte Video, I shall venture to acquaint those naval officers who have made any stay at this place (and it is a piece of intelligence which most persons would not think worth while to communicate, neither should I, if I were not certain that they are always glad to hear of the welfare of an old friend, and particularly in a distant part of the world,) that the accomplished lady who bears the cognomen of the "Rattlesnake" is still exquisitely fair, enchantingly good, and possesses, if possible, more fascination than ever. Before we had cleared the River Plate, we descried to windward a large ship bearing down upon us with all the sail she could carry. When she came within pistol-shot she hoisted Brazilian colours, and ran close alongside, with all her guns run out, ready to blow us out of the water had we chanced to have been a Buenos Ayrian, for notwithstanding we showed the English flag, they took some time to consider us, but finding out that we were, in reality, an English sloop-of war, they stood off. It appeared that when any of the Buenos Ayrian privateers fell in with a Brazilian frigate, they generally hoisted English colours in order to deceive the enemy; and as this *ruse* had sometimes succeeded, we no longer wondered at the close inspection of the *Bravagente*. The Beagle stood in for the harbour of Maldonado, where we found the island of Goritti very strongly fortified, and as some objections were made to our remaining by the Brazilian, I felt rather disappointed in not being able to have a cup of *matté* with our good friend Donna Francisco. We accordingly departed thence, and the ships made the best of their way to Rio, where we arrived somewhere about the end of May. Although this month is considered cool at Rio, still I could not find it out; perhaps having recently breathed the pure air of Paraguay, made the heat appear more oppressive, and all in our berth very soon began to exhibit evident symptoms of increased perspiration. It is not every person who has been so fortunate as to be in the Middy's berth of a ten-gun brig, and particularly in a climate where the thermometer is above 95° in the shade; but they may imagine five or six persons crammed in a small space, laying in plenty of hot soup, followed by a curry as hot as the weather, and the air, which is only admitted through the gratings of the patent bull's-eye, very often prevented from entering by some of the sailors (employed upon deck) heedlessly placing their naked feet over the ventilation; but when this was the case, we never failed to disturb them by a gentle push with a fork.

Soon after our arrival at Rio, some gentlemen from the Middy's berth of the Adventure proposed an excursion up the country in a boat, and as I was always glad of an opportunity of accompanying them (for they were most excellent companions), I obtained leave of absence for a day or two, and as they had provided abundance of provisions of acknowledged and approved flavour, we departed with great spirit and vivacity, and in less than an hour we had reached the villa of Francisco (formerly coxswain to Sir Sydney Smith, but now a getter-up of linen to the navy,) whom we had often threatened with a visit. On our arrival at his house, we soon spread ourselves over the grounds without ceremony, and coming to a spot where a number of laughing negresses were standing, above their knees in water, employed in washing (which is performed here by stamping upon the linen and afterwards beating it between large stones), we remained gazing upon these curious figures, who pursued their daily toil with many noisy splashings and evident cheerfulness. It happened that one of our party (possessed of great warmth of imagination) was seized with an inclination to be very attentive to one of the *dark* beauties, and was bold enough, considering it was his first attempt, to place his hands on each side of her sooty face, and admire the broad smile, which disclosed the usual supply of strong white teeth defending a mouth of very unusual dimensions. As his advances seemed to be favourably received by the dingy *Blanchisseuse*, we began to entertain ourselves with some of the others, and succeeded, for they were by no means averse, in promoting among them a great deal of fun, frolic, and amusement. I suppose we must have made some noise in our gambols, for in the midst of our innocent hilarity Mrs. Francisco rushed in among us, and instantly the black wenches set up a sort of halloo, and fled away with affright and terror; indeed, all of us at first thought of making a handsome retreat, but having nothing in our heads but a love of fun, we stopped to admire the angry gestures, and listen to the uproarious talk of Mrs. F., but as she could not speak English, and none of us being *au fait* at scolding in Portuguese, the beauty of the harangue was lost upon us, although we could fully appreciate the force of the delivery. This was much against our entertainment at the house; for Francisco himself arrived at the spot, and, possibly, vexed at our poaching upon his manor, and set on by his wife, began to be so unreasonable as to wish our immediate departure; and his wife even refused to make an omelet for the clerk, although he told her that he had a great *penchant* for one at that time. After some angry discussion, we thought it best to get into the boat, but we had not rowed many paces when we were all seized with an inclination for dinner, and we accordingly anchored immediately opposite to the house. Having displayed our provisions (which consisted of a turkey and ham, and a profusion of fowls and tongues, with plenty of foaming bottled ale,) to the sight of Francisco, who kept surveying us from the veranda of his house: we imagined that we could perceive him smack his lips at the abundant repast. After having made a libation of a few bottles of claret, we did not lose time in beating about, but the wind being fair we proceeded further up the country, and about five o'clock in the afternoon we made for a large bay, and ran boldly in for the shore.

The place where we now landed appeared to be the estate of some Portuguese nobleman, for, about two hundred yards upon the uplands, stood a delightful country-house, having a fine grove of orange trees in the front, with large coffee plantations and vineyards in the rear. Having left the boat in care of the men, we deemed it harmless to rest ourselves in one of the alcoves or arbours, which were interspersed about the grounds, expecting that the proprietor of this spot would shortly arrive, or send and invite us to walk in and refresh ourselves. We waited as long as our sanguine dispositions would allow, and, attracted by the odoriferous perfume of the place, we walked towards the house, but were greatly surprised by not meeting with either a José or Antonio (most slaves are so named), or hearing any hostile note either of man or beast. When we arrived at the lawn we stopped to consider the propriety of going any further; but the Devil, or the liquor, one or the other, put it into our heads to walk in (for the door stood most invitingly open) and seat ourselves in a neatly-furnished room, in one corner of which stood a large and chubby figure of St. Antonio, and a beautiful image of the Virgin Mary, which was surmounted by a costly chain, to which was affixed a crucifix of gold. Being thus self-introduced, and having admired every thing in this room, and refreshed ourselves with a draught from a calabash of fine cool water, we began to cough loudly, to apprize the inmates that they had visitors who required their attention; but the house was perfectly still, not a sound was heard, and considering that something might have happened to the family, we determined to ascertain, if possible, the cause of this inauspicious silence. On ascending the stairs we came to an elegantly furnished room, in the centre of which stood a table provided with an excellent assortment of liqueurs, and numerous bottles of orgeat, tamarina, lemonada, capillaire, and strong waters. A double-barrelled gun and a pair of red slippers, lay upon one of the chairs; a set of mosquito curtains and a formidable tobacco-pipe, graced the sofa; and the sideboard presented a quantity of glass, candlesticks, and goblets. Notwithstanding we endeavoured to set a guard upon our behaviour, yet this was a temptation not to be resisted, and therefore, without venturing a step further in search of the inmates, we arranged ourselves about the table, and passed such a busy and happy half-hour, that now there appeared some danger of the bottles being mulcted of more than one half of their contents. In the height of our enjoyment a door suddenly opened at the farther end of the room, and a thin, spare figure, wrapped in a loose dressing-gown, stalked, with great solemnity, into the apartment, and surveyed us, with a face as pale as ashes, from a mixture of consternation and fear, presenting a fine contrast to the broad gleam of satisfaction which had spread over the countenances of all our party. On the entrance of this apparition we all arose, and kept making profound bows, but he did not honour us with any salutation. At last, one of us addressed him in Portuguese, when he pronounced, with great significance of voice and gesture, *Nao entiende;* words which applied to more than one meaning, that he did not understand what we said, nor the reason of our being there. Considering silence better than attempting any explanation, we bowed again, and walked leisurely down stairs, leaving our Portuguese host immoveably fixed in the centre of the room, and, no doubt, wondering at the companionable qualities we had evinced at his expense. When we had sufficiently amused ourselves in the orangerie, we got into the boat and sailed among some small islands, upon which we sometimes landed, and proceeded to the various cottages built upon the beach, but not meeting with any novelty—for it was nothing new for us to observe, at the windows of these dirty habitations, a gross mulatto woman extracting (a pretty evening's amusement) large *piôlhos* from the heads of her young family—we sought other inland parts, which we hoped would afford both information and amusement. The night began to set in dark, when we stood into a sort of creek, which ran between large plantations, but long before we had reached the centre of it there fell a very heavy mist, which wetted us to the skin in a very short time. We began now to pull in good earnest, in order to ascertain, first, whither we had got to, and then to get shelter for the night, if there was a possibility. It now rained very hard, and shortly afterwards the boat grounded, and remained fast upon a bank. After having used vain exertions to get her off, it was agreed that I should mount on the shoulders of one of the sailors, and be carried on shore, which was at a short distance, and make inquiries for the nearest hotel. The sailor had not taken many steps when (whether my weight rendered him top-heavy, or the unevenness of the ground made him reel, I know not,) he staggered some paces to leeward, and not being able to recover his equilibrium, he fell like a dead weight. On witnessing my downfall, all those in the boat recovered their good humour, which had partly vanished as the rain descended; but for my own part, I directed my course towards some palings, which appeared to be the boundary of a small plantation, and getting over them, I was surprised to find myself by a roadside, and in the vicinity of a few miserable habitations. I was about to knock at one of them, when I observed a *pulperia* (a grog-shop), within a few yards of me; thither I soon bent my steps, and quickly ascertained, from the staring and wondering inmates, that the nearest hotel was at Praya Grande, from which place we were distant about three miles. Having made my companions acquainted with the welcome news, they hastened on shore, but in so doing they met with much the same drenching as that to which I had been subjected. As there was not the least chance of putting up at this place, we supplied the sailors with a sufficiency of grog and what provisions the pulperia afforded, and it being decided that they should remain by the boat (which was now hauled up upon the shore) while we should proceed to the Hotel Française, and as a Portuguese *de Lisboa*, who came up at the time, undertook to be our guide, we instantly set forward, telling the men we would join them the first thing in the morning. About eleven o'clock at night we arrived at the hotel, when setting our guide down to a bottle of Bourdeaux and a dish of stewed *camarões* (prawns), which stunk abominably of garlic, we went up stairs and soon forgot, in the noble carouse that followed, the disagreeables of the early part of the evening. The next morning we hurried down to the spot where we had left the boat, when we were told that a strong party of the *policia* had visited the sailors in the night, and suspecting them to be stragglers from some man-of-war, had used them rather roughly. However, the men succeeded in making them understand the true reason of their remaining, and they had at last departed, but not before they had contrived to steal out of the boat several of our mess mugs and a knuckle of ham. As I begin to fear the reader will be tired, if he is not so already, should I relate some other incidents which occurred before we returned to the ship, I shall not therefore trouble him, but merely state that we found our cruize turn out very little to our emolument, for the Brazilians find (what does not take much penetration or sagacity to discover), that the English navy make sufficient amends, and abundantly compensate for any noise, or unreasonable disturbance, which they may chance to create.

In a very few days after this trip I began to discover undoubted symptoms of a wish to seek for a little amusement among the *mônde* of St: Sebastian; and it was on a pleasant evening in the month of June that I determined to cool myself by a walk on shore. If I say I did not feel inclined to betake myself to the common resources found at the Hotel du Nord, it was because I began to tire of the monotony; and and to know the utter impossibility of gleaning any information by remaining there, as I had done formerly, swallowing bad claret and listening to the frantic mirth of the German and Brazilian officers. It was eight o'clock, and the houses and purlieus of this city were beginning to vomit forth their party-coloured and tawdrily dressed inhabitants. Already the fat and deep-bronzed mulatto, in a dress of virgin white, was to be seen waddling along in all pomp and nicety with her dark doldrum head uncovered, attended by a *sleazy* young negress, carrying a pink umbrella, with her mouth crammed full of banana, who kept gazing upon the numerous fireworks which were exploding in front of the different churches, for this happened to be a feast day, and the Rua D'ereita was one blaze of light. Many large bonfires, at certain distances from each other, burnt fiercely, and around the flaming wood gambolled a number of half-clothed mulatto and negro children. Numerous flights of rockets ascended and descended (as our showmen have it) in all parts of the city. The loud tolling of the bells, from most of the churches and convents, were intermingled with discharges of musketry, and a number of officers of almost all nations, and the dark-haired, pale-faced senhoras, attended by their families, stepped leisurely forward among the motley group, occasionally incommoded by a string of heavily-chained negroes, who came along clanking their fetters in horrible unison with the general noise and tumult. Perhaps this scene was rendered still more striking by the glare of numerous torches, which are carried by the procession of the Host, and as this approaches every one is uncovered, and all the wretched-looking beggars, as well as the *mediocre* of both sexes, fall upon their knees and remain praying until it has passed.

As I made my way through the busy multitude, I avoided the crowd by walking up another street, which presented a contrast to the scene I had just witnessed. In vain did I peer up at the windows to catch a glimpse of any of the inmates—all was still, silent, and motionless; and the only signs of occupancy which presented themselves were the forlorn negro servants, sitting on the threshold of the doors, singing the wild airs of their native land in a mournful and pleasing cadence, accompanying their voices upon an instrument of a singular construction, which sends forth a melancholy and cheerless sound. Some of these unhappy wretches play well upon the guitar, and it seems to afford them great amusement to sit at the doors of a night and pour forth their wild melody; and not unfrequently do they exhibit the strange dances of their country, enlivened by the sound of the *strum, strum,* and the music of the *banger**. As I passed by I asked one of them (in the Portuguese language) how long he had been in Rio, and from whence he came. He told me that he had been in this city ever since he was ten years of age, and that he was born a great distance *(múito longe)* from Benguela, in Africa. Upon my asking whether he had ever seen a white man at the place of his nativity, he answered in the negative; and on my wishing to know what they would do with a white man in his land, he laughed very heartily, and looking at me significantly, passed his finger across his throat. This question of mine seemed to please him very much, and I left him giggling and chuckling over the phrases of *Brazéllero nao 'sta bom—Meu terra 'sta bom—Ingleses, 'sta mucto bom.* At the end of the street I came suddenly upon a swarm of persons who were chanting and screaming before a large waxen figure, gaily festooned with lamps and wreaths of flowers. It was the vesper service.

* An instrument somewhat similar to the mandolin.

Upon this occasion they took great pains to make as much noise as possible; and as this assemblage consisted chiefly of old white-headed, bare-legged black-a-moors and dolorous-visaged mulattos, throwing up the whites of their eyes, their countenances undergoing so many changes, and their throats sending forth such jangling notes that it was enough to discompose the gravity of any virgin upon earth. A sepulchral-voiced friar rolled out the first lines of the prayer, and the "ready chorus" seemed to be made up of as many different sounds as there were persons among them.

I am fully sensible that my abilities are inadequate to the task of conveying an exact idea of the various characters I met with that evening; for now was to be seen the gaunt, long-armed, turbaned negress, swinging along with a basket of fuming savoloys, and this shoeless dealer would stop in her career to gaze at the leprous corse of a mulatto infant, which was carried upon a bier. A profusion of roses encircled the head of the child; the hands, holding a cross, were raised in an attitude of prayer;

and its mouth was stuffed full of cotton. The crab-like progression of the numerous cripples; the friars of all the different orders; the noisy slaves running to and from the public fountains, carrying upon their heads buckets of water; the ludicrous appearance of the black venders of eggs and vegetables in the different markets; and the grizzle-headed, paunchy negro women, who supply sweetmeats and aquadênte to the *canaille*, are mingled with the gay throng, and perhaps serve to set off, by their own whimsical look and dress, the true symmetry and figure of the chaste, the beauty, and the well-born, who enliven the strange promenade.

It was past midnight: the streets were partly hushed, except when the sound from the melodious guitar of the serenader broke upon the silence, and the distant trampling of the horses of the armed police, who scour the streets all hours of the night. By this time I had strolled to a remote part of the town, when, as I passed the latticed window of a small house, I heard confused sounds of people talking together in the room. As I listened attentively, I distinguished certain pathetic lamentations and doleful cries, which led me to suppose that the inmates had met upon some sorrowful occasion. I took advantage of a pause (being determined to offer my assistance if it were necessary, and knocked gently at the door, which was immediately opened by a middle-aged woman dressed in white, who first surveyed me with some scrutiny, and, to my great surprise, without any inquiry, said, "*Entré, senhor, entré.*" On my entrance, I found myself in the midst of a crowd of senhoras, and many lights were gleaming from a side table, upon which also stood some bottles and glasses, partly filled with wine; and although some kind of perfume was burning, it did not allay the strong smell of garlic and onions which pervaded the room. It is needless to mention, that I was surveyed by all present with some surprise, but they were a very polite circle, and some of them advanced with an easy gentility, and asked me, in Portuguese, if I was not an English surgeon; but without waiting for my reply, they hurried me towards a corner of the apartment, where I beheld, extended on a mattress, the shrivelled form of an old woman, who appeared to be in a dying state. Although I knew about as much of medicine as I did of measuring a curved line, yet it was easy to perceive that the old lady was in danger of suffocation, not only from the oppressive heat of the room, but also from the officious attentions of the women who crowded round the couch, and counted with great devotion the large beads of their rosaries. Into the right hand of the dying person was thrust a large image of St. Antonio, which, in her agony, she had grasped by the throat; while in the left hand she crushed a long tallow candle, which I was given to understand was placed there as a passport to heaven. Many images of Saints (some of them maimed and noseless) lay in confusion upon the bed, and the pale face of *Nossa senhora das Merces* was reclining upon the neck, more than moderately brown, of the expiring Brazilian. The reader will be mistaken if he thinks that I felt at all abashed at the novelty of my situation; but, as they seemed to solicit an exercise of my skill, I gently felt her pulse, and began to meditate, which has always a fine effect, and then my first consideration was to make the crowd fall back to the further end of the room, and the next was to order the doors and windows to be thrown open, for, to confess the truth, the apartment required a little ventilation. One of the young women, whom I afterwards ascertained to be the daughter of the sick lady, then came forward to assist me, and began to wipe the deluge of perspiration from the puckered forehead of her parent, who trembled excessively, making me think that her numerous friends had frightened her very much. I had no sooner found means to make her relinquish the candle than St. Antonio was subjected to additional pressure, for her hand, moistened by tallow, seized the legs of the Saint, and thus grasped by the head and feet she held the figure before her, and prayed to it most earnestly. Whether it was the fresh air, or some diluted wine which I gave, or the prayers to St. Antonio, I know not, but she so far recovered as to raise herself up and lay hold of me, apparently with the generous intention of an embrace, but I gently avoided the favor by restricting her to the horizontal position. As I perceived that the wine she had taken had acted as a powerful restorative, I ventured to administer a little more to her, but she had no sooner drunk it than she perplexed me very much by falling into a deep sleep or a swoon.

I recollected that Gil Blas, when he attended the grocer's son, encountered a little swarthy physician, called Dr. Cuchillo, with whom he fought, and hearing that the old lady was attended by a *Medico* equally swarthy, I began to feel uneasy, and I resolved to depart; but they would not allow me, for the daughter ordered the door to be closed, and brought me a tumbler of *vinho porto*, which she handed to me on a plate, with the sleeves of her dress tucked above her elbows. And now my view was regaled by a table well furnished with dishes of fish and stewed prawns, flanked by omelets; sausages and onions, and other messes, well garlicked, were also placed upon the tables. I do not know that I am remarkably liable to be captivated by a good supper, but I nevertheless yielded to their entreaties, and down I sat among them. As I was accommodated with a knife and silver fork (the only one the house afforded), I appeared to be singular, for the rest dexterously pinched off pieces of fish with their fingers; and there appeared to be a great advantage attached to this mode of feeding themselves, for the contents of their plates very soon vanished, and the onions were eaten as if they had been apples. But perhaps the reader will imagine that the wine did not circulate freely, that was not the case, and although they did not lose their sobriety of manners, they all drank a sufficiency to become rather noisy than otherwise, and gave me a proof of the hospitality of their dispositions, by pressing on me the delicacies of the table, and inviting me to drink; and this latter invitation, in particular, I never suffered them to repeat, for I always considered it a piece of ill manners to refuse any offers of that kind. As they seemed only to follow the dictates of their own goodnature, I made myself as free as if I had known them many years; and it may occasion some wonder when I say that they gave way to a remarkable degree of sprightliness, and the old lady seemed to be entirely forgotten, which I thought very odd. And now, perhaps, my readers may laugh at or condemn me, for I shall relate in what manner this adventure terminated, and if the latter, earnestly entreat them to act more wisely themselves on a similar occasion. I shall content myself, therefore, with this short observation to the phlegmatic and cautious, and return to my narrative. The greater part of this assembly had departed, and I was left with the daughter and a bulbous-nosed elderly lady, and we drank "potations pottle deep" in great friendship and harmony, until I began to fear I was trespassing on their civility, and I accordingly got up to go away; but thereupon ensued a round of courtesies and compliments, which, as they would be uninteresting to detail, I shall merely say, that at the conclusion the daughter of the invalid had prevailed upon me to stay, and her elderly friend busied herself in spreading upon the floor a mattress and white coverlid, and then resumed her seat at the table, after having trimmed the candles and pointed to the mattress, to signify that I might repose myself if I felt such inclination, and I was persuaded to recline upon it, for I began to feel symptoms of somnolency creeping over me. But my companions seemed determined to make a night of it, and proceeded, with astonishing vivacity, to take off a few more bumpers (which was pardonable enough, considering their spirits had been a good deal dashed); but I suppose both of them, feeling the effects of their perseverance, soon arose from the table, and the dishes being removed, the elder took off the table-cloth, which having wrapped around her, she snuffed the candles out, leaving only a small lamp burning; they then flung themselves on each side of me and fell into a deep slumber. I soon followed so desirable an example: but this was too good a situation to last long, for I was awakened in about an hour afterwards by a clattering at the window, which was quickly thrown open, and a swinging fat fellow tumbled into the room. As he appeared rather the worse for liquor, I expected that he would fall athwart the mattress, and crush the peaceful trio; but he staggered to an old sofa in one corner, and dropped upon it like a tired bullock, and after several ill-suppressed eructations he seized my straw hat (which chanced to be there), and crumpling it up, placed it under his head by way of a pillow, and with great unconcern fell asleep and snored like an Ogre. As I had, but a day or two previous, purchased my *chapeau de paille* in the Rua D'ouvidor, I was confoundedly vexed at seeing it administer to the comfort of this fine fat-headed fellow, and I felt much inclined to disturb the composure of his brawny frontispiece by smacking into it the remains of an omelet, but my attention was diverted from so rash an act by a heavy groaning, which proceeded from the sick old lady, and on looking towards her, I perceived that she struggled considerably, and by the distortions of her face I imagined there was no time to be lost for her friends to pursue the candle system. I therefore shook and jogged them with much perseverance; but all my efforts to awaken them were ineffectual, so deep were their slumbers, in consequence of the wine which they had drunk. Meanwhile, the old lady became worse; I therefore punched them about in despair, and plied my elbows quickly, which only occasioned the eldest to send forth a few low snorts, and I then continued to pummel both without mercy, but all in vain. In this dilemma, the sick old lady suddenly became as frantic as a bedlamite, and to my great uneasiness she held up her skinny arms and clenched fists, and whirled her limbs about in so strange a manner, that all the saints fell, or rather were kicked off the bed upon the floor. But I no sooner perceived her foaming at the mouth, than I jumped up in great trepidation, and with infinite hurry I withdrew my straw hat from under the head of the fat stranger, which caused his skull to fall with a heavy thump against the sofa, and taking one look at the ghastly features of the poor withered creature, I darted out of the window, leaving this habitation of the slumbering and the dying with all possible celerity.

About this time three ships from the Emerald Isle, importing more than five hundred of the "finest pisantry," came into the harbour of Rio. The Emperor of Brazil knowing that it was the most absurd thing in the world to place confidence in the bravery of his gross and superstitious subjects, and determined to have those around him upon whom he knew he could depend in case of emergency, had caused to be held out very advantageous offers to these Milesians to leave the rusticity of their native shores, and come to a land of milk and honey. These poor fellows, thinking how delightful it would be to live with such amiable people, had consequently embarked, with their wives and families, in the visionary anticipation of passing the remainder of their days in great plenty and enjoyment. It is not for me to ascertain how far these offers were but a pretext for inveigling and coaxing these fine fellows to a country where, on their arrival, they were subjected to every species of degradation and disappointment, and looked upon, by the tribe of lepers who compose the Brazilian soldiery, with an eye of jealousy and envy. To promise and perform are different things; and all very soon found, that they had not only been duped and made fools of, but that also there was every chance of being very ill clothed and worse fed, and in all probability, which in reality some months afterwards took place, knocked on the head by some of the base negroes of Congo and Angola. As it is not my intention to enter into the particulars of the tragic event which took place in the city of Rio Janeiro in June, 1828, when the Irish and German battalions, no longer able to bear indignity and ill-treatment, arose simultaneously against the Brazilians, and a fierce and sanguinary conflict ensued, during which they took ample vengeance for the brutality which, in many instances, had been exercised on their respective countrymen. I shall, therefore, only relate a few incidents which came under my observation.

About a fortnight after their arrival, I imagined that the best use I could make of an idle day would be to visit them in their quarters at Praya Vermêlha (Red Beach), and being joined at the the Hotel du Nord by one of my messmates, and also by the assistant-surgeon of the Adventure, we were about to depart, when a gentleman, who was eagerly engaged *a la fourchette* at an adjoining table, suddenly arose, and excited our curiosity, by relating some of his adventures at Praya Vermêlha; and as he had made some attempts to gain admittance, but without success, he much wished to join our party. He was a man of good stature, and appeared to be a Frenchman. He spoke well. His conversation was witty and agreeable, and his manners noble and simple, and he evidently was a person of observation, for he had a very sly manner of examining what was passing about him. As there is always an advantage in travelling with a companion who possesses understanding and information, we set out together. On our arrival we knocked loudly at the gate, which being opened by a grim-looking creature of a mulatto, the gentleman who accompanied us gave him to understand that we wished to be admitted, whereupon this sentinel soon tripped away, and having made known our application, some of the Irish gentlemen attached to the expedition presently came forward and welcomed us with much cordiality. But nothing could equal the pleasure which many of the emigrants manifested at the sight of us, for men, women, and children gathered around, and the characteristic humour of the Irish here shone in all its native and irresistible vivacity. While we testified our surprise that so fine a body of men should be made the victims of the machinations of interested persons, it was proposed by the Irish officers that we should adjourn to their quarters in the barracks and taste the whisky, some of "the real Simon Pure," an offer we readily embraced, and put in practice immediately. After passing some time in this very agreeable occupation, Moreau, for that was the name of our new acquaintance, became elated, and launched out in the praise of whisky, of which he gave an analysis, and what quantity of alcohol a quart of whisky contained; he also swore it was a great purifier of the blood, and then ended his harangue by drinking off a large glass of it and damning the Bourbons. I soon ascertained that he had been an officer in the French service, and had served under the Emperor Napoleon in many campaigns. He also told me that he had devoted some time to the study of languages, and that he was a tolerable musician. Having requested a specimen of his minstrelsy, one of the Irish officers presented him with a flute, upon which he played several of Moore's Melodies with such a melancholy and tender pathos, that all of us were quite enthusiastic in our praise. After he had executed many passages from Mozart and Rossini with a brilliancy and tone little inferior to Drouet or Nicholson, he finished with *Erin go bragh*. Soon afterwards he entered upon military affairs, and showed his skill in field tactics to Captain H——. His manœuvres were altogether lost upon me, but not upon the captain, whose attention was entirely absorbed, and Moreau and he were very shortly engaged both in column and the extended order. But we were now disturbed by a loud clamour, and we were given to understand that the men's dinner hour had arrived, and the mess was about being served out.

I have heretofore observed, that the countenances both of soldiers and sailors (at their dinner hour) look brisk and cheerful, but on descending to the place where the provisions were ready for distribution, I saw none but discontented, pale, meagre faces; and the faded complexions of some of the women, who, on their arrival, looked the picture of health and contentment, filled us with sympathy and compassion. Several of them approached me with a pail of wash intended for soup, but what had been used as a succedaneum in making it I could not discover, for it was a most nauseous mess. As one of the Irishmen, who carried a large wooden platter upon which was placed a few small pieces of beef, happened to pass, I asked him if he would not have some soup, when he exclaimed, in a very piteous tone, "To be sure, and I'll be with the Lord if I take a bowl of it;" and on my expressing a curiosity to know how he liked the beef, he immediately replied, "Taste it yourself, sir, and then you'll know all about it." I, however, was not tempted by the appearance of this dish, and therefore declined the invitation; but I endeavoured to alleviate his complaints, by pointing out the privations we were sometimes forced to undergo on board of a man-of-war; and although the present usage of himself and countrymen was discouraging, yet, in a very short time, they would possibly be well fed and receive their pay. He seemed to listen attentively to what I said, but he declared that he wished himself at home again, and told me that he bitterly regretted the day when he left "ould Ireland" to sail for Brazil; and he might have added, "May that hour stand for aye accursed in the calendar." How long these people were condemned to languish on such provisions, for even the bread looked unwholesome, I know not; but this treatment certainly induced among the Irish an antipathy against the Brazilians, which, on their arrival, existed only on the part of the latter towards themselves. They were promised much, but these promises were not of sufficient efficacy to prevent a great many from becoming distempered; and I had an opportunity of seeing a number, both male and female, extended on their miserable pallets, and destitute of every convenience necessary for people in their helpless condition. As we were departing I looked round for Moreau, when I observed him surrounded by a crowd of the emigrants, who were shaking hands with him, and many of the women ran forward and gave him several hearty kisses. I soon observed that his hand was full of milrea notes, and he endeavoured to alleviate their distresses by offers of money, but they all rejected this proof of his benevolence. Some months afterwards I ascertained Moreau to have been wandering through the country nearly destitute and *sine nummo;* but he never failed, on his approach to any habitation, to take out his flute, and his great skill in music seldom failed to procure him a lodging for the night and whatever fare the house afforded.

We this day adjourned to the French hotel at Bota-fogo, where we passed our time very comfortably, and on one of the Irish gentlemen being asked how he liked the Brazilians, he complained of the treatment which he had received, and observed that amongst other disagreeable methods of showing their enmity, they had thrown something down upon him from the windows. Upon hearing this, Moreau observed that he was not aware of the custom, for it was a decided mark of particular favour and esteem if any lady threw roses or flowers upon an individual as he passed under the veranda. The Irishman allowed the observation to be perfectly just, but, added he, with great humour, "By the holy Jasus God, there 's a deal of difference between a flower and a brickbat," for it appeared that instead of roses he had been saluted with such missiles. After having entertained ourselves like reasonable creatures (it being by this time pretty late), and prevented Moreau from strangling several Frenchmen, for we found out that he was a perfect "Alcide," we bade adieu to the Irish officers, who returned to their qaurters, and we proceeded on board, and thus ended this day's adventure, over which I lay revolving in my hammock before I fell asleep. The inhospitable reception by the Brazilians of the Irish, a people so proverbially hospitable themselves, was carried to a great length, and I could not help pitying the poor officer who received brickbats from the senhoras where he might have expected roses. However, soon afterwards I became acquainted with an officer, who, to palliate in some degree their behaviour, related an adventure, which went certainly so far as to prove that the other portion of his majesty's liege subjects were not equally out of favour with them. He had been but a short time in Rio, and was a proficient, I believe, in everything but the language. He was a great lover of the opera, and having plenty of money at his command, he on every night of performance took his seat in one of the boxes on the second tier, not from any dislike of the pit, but merely for the pleasure of being near the person of a young and beautiful senhora, who consorted with a venerable and discreet lady in the next box. As he was what is termed a good-looking fellow, and, when dressed to the best advantage, made no despicable appearance, it may be imagined that this young damsel wished to extend her conquests, for he certainly perceived that behaviour in her which he reasonably enough interpreted as an encouragement to many persuasive looks which his admiration had induced him to give her. I have said that the boxes at Rio are partitioned off; he had therefore no very convenient access to her, but as she reclined close to the partition on one side, and he on the other (through the force of attraction I suppose), their arms came occasionally in contact, but the pressure was so gentle, and so innocent, that it may be supposed the young lady was not aware of the circumstance, for she did not alter her position, but suffered her elbow to remain resting on the velvet cushion. My friend felt not a little flattered at this instance of her condescension, and while he was thinking how to bring about an assignation with this graceful beauty, she turned her face full upon him, and her eyes, "so large and languishingly dark," beamed with an expression similar to that of Widow Wadman, when she made an attack on my Uncle Toby; not that I mean to associate such an experienced campaigner as the Widow Wadman with this fascinating senhora, for she as far surpassed the widow as greatest does least. At this "leer of invitation" he felt his affection increase to such a degree, that he nearly yielded to his transports, and was almost tempted to serve the delicate arm of this innocent creature in the same manner as Tom Jones did the muff of Sophia. And now I am fearful that the reader will, when he has read the end of this adventure, blame my friend very much for his want of "tact" (vile phrase), or whatever name may be considered more suitable, for as soon as the senhora perceived the gentleman ogling her with unabated ardour and vivacity, she, with a modest deportment and downcast eyes, withdrew a diamond ring from her finger, and placed it with great circumspection and secrecy, beyond the partition, on the edge of the velvet covering of my friend's box. But, alas! his evil genius presided at that hour; for, from some unaccountable feeling (and which certainly will render him liable to a charge of stupidity), he suffered the ring to remain glittering before his eyes, and, without offering to take it up, remained gazing at it with astonishment. Whether the young lady considered herself slighted by his not immediately removing it, or fearful of discovery, I know not, but certain it was that she very quickly snatched the ring away, and having darted at my amazed friend a look of reproach and anger, she spit down by the side of her (a most sovereign mark of contempt among the Brazilians), and hid herself from view. At this unexpected behaviour my friend sunk back in his chair, and remained for the space of a few minutes overwhelmed with shame and confusion, but wishing to retrieve this sad mistake, and trusting that his case was not quite hopeless, he ventured to lean forward, and prepared to give her a most redeeming sort of ogle, but to his great regret and chagrin he found that she had quitted the box, and that her place was occupied by a lady, who in age and dress more resembled *Tamehamalu*, the Queen of the Sandwich Islands, than the beauty he was in pursuit of, only this lady was on a much larger scale, and had a *nez retroussée*, with a face of the colour of a well-burnished warming-pan, and eyes like Dame Leonarda, that "flamed in purple." In short, she was so much the reverse of the indignant unknown, that he instantly made a safe and quiet retreat, and went in search of the maiden, not doubting that if he could meet with a convenient opportunity, he should be able to bring the adventure to a favourable issue. But he found, to his great sorrow, that she had left the theatre, and although he visited the opera many times afterwards, he never saw her again.

Captain Stokes now received orders to sail from this harbour; their general tenor was, that he should proceed to Santos, on the coast of Brazil, and then make the best of his way to Paranagua, and after touching at the Island of St. Catherine, to proceed to Monte Video, and return from thence to Rio Janeiro. Being by this time well manned, the Beagle, on the 17th of June (leaving the Adventure at anchor), sailed from Rio, and without any event worthy of observation, arrived off Santos on the 21st instant. When we came in sight of the fort, they fired a gun, and we observed two vessels bearing down upon us, and in a short time we perceived the largest to be a twenty-gun ship, the other was a schooner, and her deck was literally crowded with men. On looking towards the beach, opposite the fort, we saw, to our great astonishment, numbers of people running about in the greatest possible disorder; but, nevertheless, some of them contrived to bring two or three twenty-four pounders to bear upon the Beagle, for by this time we had come within range of the fort, and sailed very quietly into the harbour. We were totally at a loss to know what all this could mean, and, indeed, were somewhat distressed at seeing them take so much trouble on our account. As the ships neared us amazingly fast, we were not long in suspense, for we were hailed by the largest ship, and having answered her inquiries, she sent her boat on board with an officer, who told us that the ship he came from was the Pampero Brazilian brig-of-war. It happened that they had mistaken us for a Buenos Ayrian privateer, for not unfrequently these privateers were cruizing off the harbour, and as they had observed the supposed Buenos Ayrian stand into the bay, they had embarked a number of men from the fort, determined to give her warm reception. It was almost impossible to help laughing at the ridiculous-looking faces of the mulatto soldiers on board of the smaller vessel; and, doubtless, all these men were very happy to find that we were peaceably inclined, for they have a very great dread of fighting, and particularly at close quarters. The "Pampero," as well as the fort, now made great despatch in saluting, and the usual number of guns were fired by the Beagle. Lieutenant Sholl, waited on the governor of the fort, to mention our intention of anchoring off the town of Santos (which lays about three miles up an arm or creek as broad as the Thames), which the governor readily permitted, but it was evident that he had not recovered his composure, for he looked very sallow and uneasy, and did not offer to Lieutenant Sholl any particular civility. When we had arrived half way up the creek, a boat came alongside, in which was the commandant (a quick and intelligent person), who coming on board, requested that Captain Stokes would not salute the fort immediately on his arrival off the town, for they were by no means prepared to return it, as the guns were out of order, but in a few hours they would be in readiness, and he would make a signal to that effect. Captain Stokes having acceded to this request, we anchored within a cable's length of the town.

In a day or two after our arrival, Mr. Kirke and myself obtained permission from Captain Stokes for an excursion into the interior of the country as far as the town of St. Paulo, which is reckoned distant from Santos about twelve or thirteen leagues. Early in the morning we went on shore, but after the most persevering efforts we were unable to procure horses, and we therefore proceeded to the house of Senhor Whittaker, his Britannic majesty's vice-consul, and meeting there with a Mr. Kilkenny, who officiated as his clerk, he kindly offered to direct us to a person who kept good horses, and he advised us to be well mounted, as it was generally considered a tedious journey. We accordingly passed through the neat and quiet town of Santos about a mile into the country, where we entered a house inhabited by a tall, thin figure of a Portuguese, and a capacious-bodied woman of the middle age, and at the end of the room sat a swarthy young man picking his fingernails with a silver-handled dirk or knife, which he quietly on our entrance put into his bosom. Mr. Kilkenny soon explained the nature of our visit; but they could or would not muster any *mulas* that day, but at seven o'clock the next morning they would be ready. Having no alternative, we closed with him for the morrow, and with some feeling of disappointment, we proceeded back to Santos, and passed the remainder of the day in viewing the town. The general appearance of the streets was clean and healthy, and the inhabitants appeared to be quiet and inoffensive. The Rua D'ereita is the best and longest street, for the houses are generally two stories high; and I was extremely glad to perceive that the ladies do not here, as at Rio, keep themselves screened from observation, but seem to have a wish to exhibit their pleasing faces to the view of Englishmen; indeed, the ladies of Santos are really handsome and well-behaved. There appeared to be very few padrés in this town, at least I saw but two or three, and one of them was a cheerful paunchy-looking fellow, and had a face puffed out like a glassblower.

Most of the churches are of extremely plain architecture, and neither rich in gilding nor plate. There is no hotel, but many better sort of *pulperias* are to be found in all parts of the town. The campo or square is not large, and in some places was covered with grass. I soon had an opportunity of becoming so far acquainted with the inhabitants as to ascertain that their minds were entirely given to mercantile pursuits, and that no person had been guilty of making any collections in zoology, mineralogy, botany, or conchology, their knowledge being confined to the price of sugar, the rate of exchange, or the means of smuggling a cargo of *matté* safe to Buenos Ayres; but when I learnt there was not a Scotchman in the town or vicinity, I began to fear that Santos could not be a very desirable or improving settlement. The militia were numerous, and were oftentimes seen crawling about the town, and most of them appeared to have been born with a cigar in one hand and a bottle of *aquadente* in the other.

On the following morning we were told that

Mr. Whittaker was that day to accompany Captain Stokes and Lieutenant Sholl to St. Paulo; therefore Mr. Kirke and myself determined to precede them, and we accordingly set off to the habitation of the Portuguese muleteer. We were given to understand, the day previous, that the ride to St. Paulo generally occupied two days; and that, moreover, we should require a guide, also that the roads were sometimes dangerous on account of the runaway negroes, who found a safe retreat in the surrounding forests, and sometimes practised a little robbery and murder upon travellers to and from Santos; and we likewise received a hint to keep clear of any Brazilian soldiery whom we might chance to meet upon the tramp towards St. Paulo, for such people were as much to be dreaded as the runaway slaves. By the time we arrived at the muleteer's it was eight o'clock, and being provided with tolerable ponies we trotted off to get breakfast at Cubertam, a town three good leagues from Santos, and where our Portuguese friend told us we should meet with every convenience and luxury. The apprehension of not meeting with a good breakfast at Cubertam would certainly have had its effects upon our spirits; but as it was, we set forward in the joyful anticipation of superior accommodation, which had such an effect upon the buoyant spirits of Mr. Kirke, that he dashed off at a quick canter, and I now found that he was far better mounted than myself; for the mule on which I rode had a plaguy rotundity of stomach, inasmuch that I found it impossible to keep my legs in a comfortable attitude, for they flew out on each side in an oblique and graceless manner.

The morning was beautifully fine, and the road, which is excellent, is on each side encompassed by thick and impenetrable forests, and numerous rivers intersect the country for miles around. We passed over a well-made wooden bridge thrown across a rapid stream (which, indeed, forms an island upon which Santos is built). As we were approaching to cross the bridge, our attention was arrested by a ragged negro boy, having on his head a basket filled with some kind of provision, who told us that he had been sent forward as our guide, but not wishing the assistance of this sable conductor, we told him to return; but as he said that he lived at St. Paulo, and was then on his way, we threw him some vinteens, which made the poor creature grin with delight. There are some huts built by the side of this bridge, and the inmates support themselves by fishing and growing mandiaca, depending a good deal upon the orange, plantain, and banana which grow spontaneously here. Every person we met upon the road invariably took off his hat, although we could willingly have dispensed with this polite custom, for our arms fairly ached, and my straw hat was compressed into various forms. After riding some time, we inquired of some peasantry how far it was to Cubertam: the answer was, "Two leagues." We therefore rode briskly forward for half an hour, when meeting a party of muleteers we made the same inquiry, and these people said that Cubertam was "two leagues and a half." About a mile from this party we met others, who now said that Cubertam was "three leagues distant." These answers not meeting our ideas of progression, we set forward at a good round pace, and in twenty minutes came to another wooden bridge, extending across a swift river, of considerable breadth, on the other side of which, we gladly ascertained, was the anxiously sought Cubertam. On passing over the bridge, a wan mulatto sentry referred us to a small house, a good deal in the style of our toll-gate, at which place a corpulent Portuguese demanded fourteen vinteens for a passport. We took this opportunity of stating our intention of reaching St. Paulo that day, and also of getting breakfast at Cubertam; and judging, from the bluff and florid look of this keeper of the toll-gate, that he was familiar with the best eating-houses, we asked him to direct us accordingly. In answer to this request he observed, that Cubertam, as long as he recollected it, could never boast of a hotel for accommodation, and was at all times, particularly for an epicure, badly provisioned. The well-fed look of our informant certainly somewhat belied the assertion. However, that we might not linger under the torments of uncertainty on this point, he called his servant and told him to precede us into the town, and assist in obtaining such delicacies as the place afforded. On our approach to it, "though no ghost, we might have taken his word for a thousand," we found the town to consist of about one hundred miserable huts, wretchedly built of sticks and poles, and the inhabitants the undoubted representatives of extreme poverty. On making application at one of the hovels, pointed out as one usually found to be the best provisioned, we had the mortification to discover that neither coffee nor bread, nor, in fact, any thing was obtainable; and after being for some time bandied about from one house to another, we found to our discomfort that success was not to be expected. We then thought of proceeding further, but on being told that the intermediate villages between Cubertam and St. Paulo were in infinitely worse circumstances, we, as a last resource, entered a filthy-looking cabin, where a party of muleteers were regaling themselves off fried pork and farina, which, however, sent forth such a savoury odour to persons in our famished condition, that we soon came to the determination of requesting the host to furnish us with a rich mess of the same, for our appetites by this time were whetted to a clamorous anxiety; and on being told that in half an hour this said tantalizing dish would be ready, we sauntered forth to view the town. Before most of the doors were seated women of a meagre and dejected appearance, and some of these tawny creatures were employed in the disgusting manner I have before had occasion to notice, which induced the wish that I could extend to them the benefit of some ivory instrument to facilitate their labours. Smoking tobacco seemed to be also a favourite amusement, for many of these women had a cigar in their mouths, and kept watching their dusky children, who were frisking about, almost in a state of nudity, among the muleteers and mules, for nearly five hundred mules at this time were resting in the square. These useful animals were laden with *arobas* of sugar, which are sent from St. Paulo, and generally make the journey in two days. A great many of the muleteers were armed with a brace of pistols, and all had a long knife stuck in a belt on the right side of the back. They are thus armed to protect them on the road; for they told us of a robbery and murder committed a year or two before, and ever since then they had travelled in the manner described. The character of these muleteers is belied by their appearance, which is ferocious in the extreme; for their scowling dark visages shaded by large straw hats, their cloaks scarcely long enough to conceal the pistols and long knife, and some having a huge cutlass dangling by their sides without a sheath, gave them more the appearance of banditti than a harmless and civil people, for such they are, and such we found them on our journey. The inhabitants of the square at this time presented a very novel appearance, and we here met with a great variety of vagabonds running about bareheaded and without either shoes or stockings, and it is amusing to observe the very tattered and torn of society treat each other with extraordinary ceremony, never failing on meeting to exchange compliments, by raising their hats (should they happen to have one) and bowing for some time reciprocally. A lame old negro leaning on his crutch (with one of his legs as thick as a mill-post, and bandaged with dirty cloths, and the other leg blessed with a lateral curve) would stop to exchange a polite morning salutation with a mulatto woman, her hair (escaping from beneath the folds of a red striped cotton handkerchief bound round her head) hung half way down her back, and carrying in one hand a wicker basket filled with oysters and sugar-cane, and in the other a bundle containing bananas and plantains. Many young girls, of a yellow and copper hue, were standing in the square, showing their dirty, yet small and pretty, feet, and talking in a loud tone to the muleteers; and I also saw many black wenches amusing themselves by tearing the rind from the sugar-cane with their conspicuously white teeth, and afterwards sucking the juice with great satisfaction. The ordinary provisions are dried fish, oysters, dried beef, pork, eggs, farina, and aquadente.

Having returned to our rendezvous, for I will not call it an hotel, we were supplied with a greasy and smoking dish of pork and farina, and a few biscuits and oranges were also set upon the table. The knives and forks seemed to have been "slubbered through the general knife-cloth," but this we soon remedied. We seemed to attract the attention of every person, and I have no doubt they considered us to be of extraordinary look and appearance—it was quite reciprocal. Our host, naturally loquacious, told us, with much indifference, that an Englishman lived within a few doors; rejoiced at this, we immediately started up and walked to his house (which was two stories high) and were so lucky as to meet him coming out of the door. He regretted not having sooner heard of our arrival, and as he informed us that he was then coming in search of us, we were exceedingly glad to prevent him any trouble of that kind. To his inquiries about our accommodation, we confessed the extremity to which we were reduced; the unacceptable feast of farina and pork, at which relation he laughed heartily; and he then said, that being perfectly aware of the entertainment we should meet with, he had prepared a breakfast, which was now ready, and only waited our arrival. As I thought he spoke in a very sensible manner, in order to show how much we valued his attention, we thanked him for his politeness, and accepted his invitation. After passing an hour at breakfast very agreeably, we bade adieu to Mr. Smith (who, by the by, was a Dane) and his good hospitality, and mounting our mules again, set forward on our journey.

After leaving Cubertam, the roads began to get bad, and by the time that we arrived at the foot of the Serra it had become very rugged and uneven. The height of this mountain is said to be nearly four thousand feet, and the ascent to the top is reckoned at two leagues. Here we had to trust to our mules, who seemed to understand the business they were upon, by the energy and sagacity with which they pursued this rugged and winding track, bounded by precipices, and obscured frequently by so dense a mist, that we were compelled to stop until it had cleared away. The mournful dashing of the waters, that rush in torrents down the various cliffs and through the caverns, cause a romantic and gloomy feeling. In some of the many and narrow defiles we frequently met companies of mules, laden with sugar, descending by slow and cautious steps, and unless you are careful in passing them, it may be productive of mischief, for I was more than once nearly thrown down by their coming in contact with me, for the mules, on meeting you, crowd close together, and descend very rapidly; consequently, such a collision would be much better avoided. The sharp-visaged muleteers were very civil, and gave us many *vivas*, so habitually ceremonious, that I believe if either of us had rolled down a precipice, it would have been attended with a "*Viva*, senhor," and the head uncovered. I have said that they are a most savage-looking set, but we had nothing to fear from their long knives; but the heavily-laden mules gave us every annoyance. Within a mile of the summit you have an extensive view of the surrounding country, and Santos, *à la distance*, appears a compact and pretty town. Various combinations of rivers are seen spreading and meandering in all directions, but I cannot say that

> "Here Ceres' gifts in waving prospect stand,
> And nodding tempt the joyful reaper's hand,"

for nothing meets the eye but forests of trees, displaying a wildness of country, and such a depth of woods, that agriculture is quite out of the question, and impracticable. Half way up the Serra my mule stopped, and all my beating and banging was of no avail; not a step further would she move. At this time some muleteers passed, and one of them, taking a whip from his pocket, applied it so successfully to the sides of the animal, that her obstinacy was soon overcome. I purchased this convenient whip, but he told me that the *mula* was *no 'sta bom*, and would not reach St. Paulo that evening. On reaching the highest point of our journey, there is a low hamlet, at which you may obtain some *quæso* (cheese) and *aquadente*.

The descent of the Serra proved far less troublesome, and the surrounding country and roads were wild and irregular; for not unfrequently did the road descend through deep and narrow defiles, where the overhanging woods being lofty, and the branches thickly interwoven, threw a deep obscurity around, and rendered the path dreary and romantic. As we rode along this silent pass, we observed a large cross erected in a cleft of the rock; it had been roughly made, and was fast mouldering to decay. Not a great distance from this spot another large crucifix met our sight, but in a much better condition than the former, and we now recollected the circumstance of the murder told us by the muleteers at Cubertam; and as the Portuguese generally erect a cross upon the spot where such a crime has been perpetrated, in all probability this was the place selected for the purpose, for the intricacies of the surrounding thickets afforded a safe rendezvous for lurking desperadoes. At an angle of the road, and just after we had merged from this fearful spot, we came suddenly upon a small detachment of mulatto soldiers at their bivouac. They were without shoes, and apparently unarmed. Some were asleep, while others amused themselves by playing at cards and smoking cigars. As we rode past, they took no other notice of us than merely begging a few vintins. Soon afterwards we came to an open view of the country, and a few low thatched houses on the brow of a hill (the trees for the space of two hundred yards having been cleared away for cultivation), and a demure negro wench, balancing upon her head a basket of eggs, and strolling towards the low hamlets, were the only objects which met our sight for some miles. The next village, I forget the name, consists of three or four houses, where the inhabitants, particularly in their cooking, are disgusting and nauseous, and we also observed a few disagreeable-looking hamlets in the vicinage. After leaving this place, we fell in with a Brazilian settler, who *existed*, I can scarcely say lived, at Fricasee, another *poor* village, notwithstanding its savoury name, a few miles from the one we had just quitted. On our arrival, the Brazilian undertook to provide some refreshment for ourselves, and he therefore placed before us some hard boiled eggs and cheese, which he pronounced to be *'sta bom;* but to the mules he threw several pumpkins, which these animals seemed to consider very succulent and refreshing. Upon inquiry, we found that in travelling it is usual to give them no other provision; indeed, they liked the pumpkins better than the dry Indian corn, which was left untouched.

The sorry animal upon which I rode, at this place seemed much inclined to remain, and as I had borne throughout the day, with some fortitude, the stubborn whims of this precious *mula*, I had no wish to risk his humour any further, particularly as the evening had set in, and we were still three good leagues from the city. I accordingly made application to the brazallero, who undertook to furnish me with a better. In a few minutes he produced a "a high trotting horse," curveting and whisking about a long tail in such a manner, that I almost regretted asking for one, for I was rendered so fatigued by the uneasy pace of the mule, that I felt more inclined for the "lady's pony" than this fiery Bucephalus. Bidding adieu to our host, we pursued our journey, and putting our horses to a heavy canter for an hour, we gladly listened to the distant sound of the bells from the churches of the city; but the ascent of rockets and other fireworks, together with the explosion of guns, proclaimed that some rejocing was going forward at St. Paulo, the cause of which we had yet to ascertain.

As we entered the square, up went a flight of rockets, loud *vivas!* were screeched out by a numerous concourse of the polite natives and ragged mulattos, and other members of the garlic-eating rabble were running about with light tapers in their hands. Pistols and muskets were fired, and most of the windows were gaily festooned with lights. In a word, there was a vast vociferation, and a number of strange and ludicrous figures, of both sexes, were spectators of these rejoicings before the large figure of a saint, which was exhibited, glittering with tinsel and robed in white, on one side of the square. It was the *Festa de St. Joao* (Feast of St. John). A great many of the better sort of people were standing before the doors of their houses, and the young ladies of the family appeared to have a great deal of good nature, for they were laughing and talking with some jovial-looking padres, and we observed other priests walking about, folded in their long black garments, who evidently preferred the noise and clamour of the square to the dreary silence of the cloisters of the cathedral. We had no sooner arrived in the centre of the place than we were surrounded by a number of the ragged bawlers, who carried the torches, and they seemed glad of an opportunity of showing their zeal before two strangers, for they renewed the shouts of '*Viva St. Joao*.' In a mischievous moment, a horizontal rocket, or *buscape*, whizzed along the ground, and exploded with a loud noise under my horse's feet, and in an instant I had disappeared off his back, for the animal gave a most fearful plunge, and I was so unfortunate as to come to the ground in a very humiliating manner. Nevertheless, I was concerned to see a tall, straw-hatted Guy Faux looking fellow, at whose feet I had fallen, instead of assisting me to rise, start back several paces, as if he had received a kick in the mouth, no doubt frightened at such an unexpected event. But I got upon my feet, and offered no apology for the fright I had occasioned him. On looking round for Mr. Kirke, I perceived him riding furiously after a shoeless mulatto boy, who was running away in great terror, with his ragged hair flying about in confusion. The people in the square gave way on all sides, and so eager was Mr. Kirke to come up with the scared runaway, that I verily believe he would have trotted over St. John had he stood in the way. Nevertheless, the urchin escaped, and Mr. Kirke came to my assistance, when he told me that the boy he had been chasing was the person who threw the rocket. Meanwhile I had been making inquiries for the French hotel (the house we had been directed to put up at), for I suffered much pain, and not being able to raise my arm from my side, I was fearful that I had dislocated my shoulder. On stating thus much to my friend, he, as well as myself, made repeated inquiries for Senhor Jaques, but we had the mortification to find, that no person knew him or the French hotel. For the space of half-an-hour did we remain surrounded by these tender-hearted people, endeavouring to make them understand, but all to no purpose; their attention was absorbed in the contemplation of the fireworks, which glided through the air; and our voices were frequently drowned in the din of the musketry, and the loud outcries of *Viva St. Joao.* At this period a Portuguese approached, who, fortunately for me, was not so crazed and lunatic as those we had been speaking to, for he exactly comprehended our dilemma, and, taking the horses by the bridles, he beckoned us to follow him; an intimation I obeyed with great good-will, for the pain of my arm had become almost excruciating. In a few minutes we arrived at the hotel, and on the appearance of Senhor Jaques I made him acquainted with my mishap, and asked him to fetch a surgeon. At the name of surgeon he appeared much alarmed, and eagerly inquired, "Vat de matter?" then holding up the candle to my face, he, with a woful countenance, exclaimed, "By Gar! you look so pale." He then alarmed the family, and forward rushed his Portuguese wife and servants, and I was led upstairs to an excellent apartment. By the time I had finished a large tumbler of wine and water, I felt greatly revived; and on asking for Monsieur, I was told that he had gone for a *médico*. He returned in a short time, and requested me "To go to my sleep for a leetel time," as the surgeon had gone into the country, but would return in something less than three hours. I cannot refuse myself the satisfaction of declaring, that the attentions I received from the honest Frenchman and his wife, were so humane and beneficial, that even if I had been their son I could not have met with greater kindness. In about an hour, to our surprise, the doctor attended, and on examining my arm he smiled, and said, *Nada, nada,* (nothing, nothing); but I was not so credulous as to believe him, for my shoulder was much swelled, and the pain extended to my fingers' ends. I endeavoured to convince him that my arm would be the better for a little pulling and hauling; but he laughed and shook his head, and still exclaimed, *Nada! nada! nada!* During this altercation, Mr. Kirke paced the room with rapid strides; the Frenchman's wife held up her hands and exclaimed, *Pobre Inglèse* (poor Englishman), and the Frenchman stared in my face without uttering a syllable. As I continued to differ with the surgeon, who laughed at my incredulity, he took his departure, having first ordered me to bed, and telling the Frenchman he would send me an embrocation. In this melancholy plight I lay down sufficiently out of humour, and for a length of time I was in great torment, but suddenly my shoulder righted with a slight snap, and I was no longer uneasy. Allowing that I had been inclined to sleep, it would have been impossible, for there proceeded from beneath the window such a confusion and hallooing, of *Viva St. Joao,* and the firing resounded through the streets in concert with the rattling of drums, the tolling of bells, and the shrill *vivas* of the delighted multitude, that I was fain to imbibe a sufficiency of *vinto* to enable me to withstand such a visitation; for I did not believe the inhabitants of such a retired place as St. Paulo would be guilty of carrying their feast-days to such a pitch of noisy extravagance.

As we had mentioned to our host that Captain Stokes and other gentlemen were on their road, and in all probability would shortly arrive, he busied himself in making every preparation, and he frequently entered the room, in great anxiety, to acquaint us with their non-arrival—a circumstance we began to wonder at ourselves, for it was now late. The next morning I much regretted my inability to attempt a journey to the gold mines within ten miles of the place; but I did not wish to prevent Mr. Kirke from proceeding—he, however, declined going by himself. At breakfast we were made acquainted, that the population of St. Paulo was in proportion of fifteen women to one man; and that the padres behaved with energy and discretion. And their conduct will appear so much the more commendable when I declare that they are solely animated by a love of religion and morality, as every person will allow when they know, that three-fourths of their time is passed among the women; and not unfrequently does the "lascivious pleasing of the lute" cheer the good men in their lonely cell. If a lady falls into a fit of melancholy, she sends for a padre. Should a padre be oppressed *à la Chuny* (the elephant), he sends for a lady, and thus do the padres pass their time in a manner which justifies a presumption that their complexion and habits are exceedingly devout, ***not at all licentious***. Indeed, I heard say that they were particularly remarkable for instances of self-denial. Mr. Kirke and myself sallied out soon afterwards, in the expectation of meeting a number of smiling faces, with sloe-black eyes and flowing locks, and we beat up successively every street in the town; but I suppose the ladies must have been engaged with their padres, for, if I remember aright, we saw none but old women trudging about. Sometimes a small lilly-white hand would be waved through the latticed window, and a gentle voice would exclaim, *Ah, Inglèses!* which salutation we would acknowledge by a piteous—ah, Senhóra!

The houses in this city are plain, generally two stories high, and have a light appearance. The churches are heavy, and not built in the best style of architecture. The streets are clean, and the temperature of at this time was 65°. As we wandered some distance out of the town, Mr. Kirke recollected that there was then residing in it an English gentleman (whose name I am ashamed to say that I now forget), who had made some valuable researches in botany, which science he pursued with unwearied perseverance, being constantly in the adjacent woods. As we had an inclination to call upon him, it was first requisite to know in what part of the town he resided, and with the intention of ascertaining it, we walked towards a number of sparkling-eyed senhoras, whom we observed parading before the doors of a handsome house. Approaching, therefore, with as genteel an air as possible, (Mr. Kirke turned out his toes, and divested himself, *pro tempore*, of the rolling walk of a seaman, and for myself I must have looked interesting with my arm in a sling,) we inquired for the *casa* (house) of Senhor ——. After some consideration, one of the young ladies tripped towards the window, at which was seated a venerable-looking don, with his head buried in a brown woollen cap, to whom she made known our application, When we came near him, he observed us attentively, and without speaking a word he threw himself back in his chair, with his head lolled upon one side, his mouth askew and open wide enough to exhibit a few decayed fangs, and closing one eye, with the other he looked up at the ceiling for some time, as if endeavouring to recollect the person. But what gave me a lively idea of the estimation in which talent is looked upon, or understood, at this place was the circumstance of this celebrated botanist being designated by the old gentleman *un pintador* (a painter), for suddenly recollecting himself he called a mulatto servant, and directed him to show us the house of the *pintador*.

Having thanked this enlightened don for his civility, and bowed to the ladies, we followed our conductor, and on arriving at the house of Mr. ———, he, unfortunately for us, was not at home, and we were consequently prevented from acquainting him with the agreeable cognomen bestowed upon him, and which, doubtless, would have occasioned him some mirth.

Having occasion for a black silk handkerchief, I made inquiries for a *mercador* (for there are not too many shops or *vendas* in this town), and one being pointed out, we walked towards the house. On our entrance, the master was happily engaged in playing at cards with some others, and he did not seem much inclined to leave the game to sell his goods. This man was a general dealer, for his shop was festooned with fiddles and guitars. He sold sugar, cheese, boots, hats, skyrockets, and rein-deer tongues. Candles (four, six, and ten to the pound,) were dangling above our heads, and a few *papagaio's de papel* (kites) were waving to and fro by the side of them. The shelves were nobly supplied with checked cotton and amber beads for the negresses, and black veils, flounced dresses, silk stockings, and gay shoes for the senhoras. There were numerous scented oils, from *à la rose double* to *mille fleurs* or *jasmin*, and, O, rare merchant, a few bottles of Day and Martin's japan were also arranged for sale. How different are the shopkeepers of Brazil from those in England. In London, such is the happy ingenuity of the tradesmen, that should you enter his shop for the purpose of buying a particular article, and he does not happen to have it, the master, by his persuasive tongue, induces you to purchase other commodities, which at your entrance you had not the slightest intention of buying. But in Brazil it is different, for they seem careless whether you purchase or not; at all events, it is neither their assiduity or civility that will tempt you to deal with them. We now returned to the hotel, expecting to find our captain and suite; but they had not arrived, and twenty surmises occurred to our minds of what might have caused their delay, and after bothering ourselves by wondering for three hours, we came to the determination of returning the next day, although my arm was still bad enough. The honest Frenchman had already provided dinner, and I imagined that he never would have ceased removing our plates, for he kept continually bringing in such a variety of viands, that we were obliged to beg him to desist. Had we met with such a supply in the Straits of Magellan, we never should have complained, but at St. Paulo this ceremonious profusion far exceeded our wishes. Having dined, our communicative host, to give a zest to the wine, told us that the prison then contained a negro who had committed eleven murders, and that one was marked by great atrocity. As we expressed a desire to hear the particulars, he gratified our curiosity by a recital of the following story.

"About four years ago (he commenced) there lived happily together, within a short distance of St. Paulo, a Branco and his wife; and as it is customary to have a favourite slave, they had selected from amongst the rest of their black servants a negro in whom they placed much confidence, and named him Joaquim. Now, Joaquim was a villain; but with that cunning and sagacity well known to exist among the negroes of Angola, he contrived to pass, in the house of his master, as a mild and inoffensive person, and he was generally considered to be of a meek and obliging disposition. In many instances, however, there was not only missing from off the estate a quantity of poultry, but, occasionally, a pig or a sheep would be found slaughtered, and a few turkies were sometimes prevented from practising their noisy gobblings by having their necks twisted in a very singular manner. Although every precaution had been resorted to by the police and others, in order to discover this midnight destroyer, still the perpetrator remained undiscovered, and for a long time the Branco was apprehensive of an attack upon himself and family, and kept upon his guard accordingly. Early one morning, the Branco went out to look over his grounds, but what was his horror on beholding the corpse of a mulatto girl (an attendant on the family) stretched upon the ground, with her head almost severed from her body. He instantly gave the alarm, and, as may be supposed, every exertion was made by himself and servants in going in pursuit of the murderer, in which Joaquim joined. But notwithstanding the police aided in the hue and cry, no trace of the assassin could be found. Not a great while after this sad occurrence, another singular and fatal attack was made upon the hens and chickens; and in the morning, when this was discovered, it was also found that Joaquim had disappeared from the house. Then, and not till then, did suspicion fall upon him. Many weeks had passed without any tidings of Joaquim, when, one morning (as the Branco and slaves were engaged on the grounds of the *chacra* (farm), and his wife was busied in her household affairs), the negro suddenly rushed into her presence. I shall not mention the proposal Joaquim made to her, but she endeavoured for a long time to dissuade him from his brutal purpose, by reminding him of the many kindnesses he had experienced in the family. It was of no avail; Joaquim proceeded to force, which she resisted for a long time, although then *enceinte*, and kept screaming for assistance. As her defence was obstinate, he drew a knife, and severely lacerated her hands and arms, and having inflicted other severe wounds, he left her in a state of insensibility. In this piteous condition she was found by her husband, who, on hearing the name of the villain who committed the outrage, rushed to the town and gave the alarm; and such was the persevering search made in every quarter, that Joaquim was taken, after a desperate resistance, and lodged in the prison. When there, he confessed to have committed eleven murders, and amongst others, to the assassination of the mulatto girl, after having violated her person. The husband proceeded to Rio Janeiro, in the hope of obtaining an order for the hanging of this precious miscreant; but his application could not be attended to, for murder is a crime not punishable by death in this part of the world, and after a great expense and loss of time, he returned to St. Paulo, where he died soon afterwards of sheer mortification. The widow," continued the Frenchman, "is now alive, and resides a few short miles from this town. She is a cripple for life, having some of her fingers cut off each hand during her conflict with the black. I have not the least doubt you may be permitted to see this praiseworthy slave, if you have curiosity enough to go to the gaol; and about this time," said the host, pulling out his watch, "the officer of the guard is at the prison."

As I was willing to see this "best o' the cut-throats," I forthwith sallied out; but I was not so fortunate as to gain admission, for they told me it was *múito tarde* (very late), but if I came in the morning, I should be admitted, an offer, I regret to say, I could not accept. As I am fond of amusement, Mr. Kirke and I sauntered about the town; but we did not find many persons abroad, and although only nine o'clock, the streets were miserably deserted and dull. On this evening, so unlike the previous one, there were no persons either to pity or admire, and we seemed to have the liberty of the whole city, through which we ranged, notwithstanding the darkness as well as silence of the streets. When we had sufficiently wondered what could have possessed the inhabitants to remain in doors upon such a fine night, and without passing much more time in tramping about, we were on our return to the hotel, when we perceived that we were followed by several tall persons, wrapped or rather rolled in long cloaks, who seemed to be actively watching us. We had already crossed the street to avoid them, when we encountered a set of gentry, who were talking with great warmth and smoking cigars. There is something unpleasant in meeting with strangers thus muffled up in sombre garments, considering that you may be certain that a long knife is concealed beneath them; but as these individuals honoured us with a *viva* as we passed, I asked one of the party what had become of all the senhoras. At this question, these talkative senhors laughed outright, and in a jocose manner told me that at that hour they seldom appeared abroad, unless upon particular occasions. I told them, that in England it was a very different affair, for there you met ladies at all hours of the night; indeed, there is such a contrast throughout the Brazils, that the difference cannot fail to strike the curious traveller, for I dare venture to affirm, that an individual might walk about the towns of St. Sebastian, St. Paulo, and Santos for months, and not be spoken to *first* by a courtezan of any complexion or colour; " Think of that,

Master Brook, think of that!" Having performed the ceremony of bidding them good night, we returned to the hotel.

Captain Stokes not having arrived, we deemed it certain some accident had befallen the party, which determined us to set off very early in the morning, although our host used many arguments to persuade us to remain. At supper, I was informed that a negro boy was making inquiries for us, and on descending the stairs, to my surprise, I found our guide had arrived, who on seeing me approach made several low bows. Guessing by this behaviour what he came about, I made the little sweepy fellow very happy in his mind, and he ran away capering with pleasure—*couchant* or *levant*, we must pay. When we had finished supper, the conversation, for want of a better subject, turned upon robbery and murder, when our vivacious landlord (and he is too good an authority to doubt) again amused us by a narration, which I shall here take upon myself to introduce.

"A Portuguese, who resided at a chacra at

the foot of some mountains, no considerable distance from St. Paulo, had occasion to visit the neighbourhood of this town, in order to arrange some dealings with another settler, about which there had been a misunderstanding. Be that as it may they quarrelled, and after much abuse on both sides, the Portuguese, as he departed ill satisfied, muttered a good deal about cheat and rogue, which expressions the other did not seem to take to himself, and they parted without his being apparently at all disconcerted. Nevertheless, the Portuguese had not quitted the house many hours before the settler seized a long Spanish gun and ammunition, and thus provided he set out for a retired path in the woods, through which he knew the Portuguese must pass on his way home. In this concealed situation he remained *five days* waiting the return of his victim, who having other visits to make about the country did not arrive sooner, when, as he rode past the spot where his *friend* was secreted, he fell dead on the other side of his mule, killed by a charge of shot which shattered his head. For this *cool* and deliberate atrocity the settler was doomed to irons and repentance for the rest of his days."

It was no sooner day than we prepared for our departure, and by ten o'clock we had quitted St. Paulo. I had confined my arm close to my side by tying round my waist a black silk handkerchief, but this contrivance did not prevent my suffering great pain and inconvenience from the motion of the horse, for we rode briskly, and in due time arrived at Fricasee. I here exchanged the white horse for my sorry mule, and as the host seemed to be a good-tempered fellow, and expressed some sympathy (a rare quality in this part of the world) for my mishap, I paid him for the hire of his horse so far beyond his expectations, that not only he, but his wife gave us a very gracious reception. We tarried here but a short time, and again set forward cheerfully; and we had scarce gone two leagues when, at a turning of the road, we came suddenly upon Captain Stokes, who was accompanied by Mr. Whittaker, Lieutenant Sholl, Mr. Mogg, purser, and another gentleman, all on high-trotting horses. Notwithstanding we were punctual to our leave of absence, (for I was always fond of returning in time, not having broken leave above four or five times since the ships left England,) yet I could have wished that we had met them a little nearer to St. Paulo, for then our leave would possibly have been extended for a day or two longer, but as we were then as near to Santos as St. Paulo, it was as advisable to proceed to the former place. The journey from Santos had occupied them two days (which accounted for their not arriving sooner), and after we had waited a sufficient time, and answered some questions concerning our journey, we finally departed, and rode some time without abating our pace.

In an obscure corner of the road we observed a number of mules resting, and the muleteers were erecting some tents, as if they were about to halt for the day. It was a very busy scene, and while some of them were making a fire others were preparing a dinner, and this employment they seemed to undertake with vast pleasure.

Having gazed at these swarthy drivers, we again set forward at a good pace, and I began to flatter myself with the agreeable idea of reaching Santos without any further mischance, when my mule suddenly fell, and I flew over her head with great despatch, and saluted the ground with a thump, which had well nigh put an interdict upon my travelling any further that day. The mule having rolled over and over got upon her legs in a twinkling, but I was in no hurry to rise, and I therefore reclined on the ground, covered with dust and sand. As I perceived by Mr. Kirke's face that he was only prevented from laughing by the apprehension of my being seriously hurt, I quickly undeceived him, and he freely indulged in a loud guffaw, with such a hearty good will that I could not resist joining in concert, and this duet was continued some time, to the great astonishment of a poor negro girl, who happened to pass at the moment. By the time we reached Cubertam it was dark, and as I found that I could not from fatigue keep pace with Mr. Kirke, I requested him not to wait for me, but to ride on and I would follow at my leisure. As soon as I had rested a short time, and given some rude assaults to a bottle of old port furnished me by the keeper of the toll-gate, I once more pursued my road to Santos.

The night was extremely dark, and swarms of fire-flies flitted across the path, occasionally emitting bright rays from their splendid lamp. I met no travellers upon the road; but I had not proceeded more than a league and a half when I saw a great light, which did not appear to be far off. As I approached I found the light to proceed from the fires of a party of muleteers, who had halted for the night on the road-side. They were in great numbers, and some were very busy in preparing supper, and they did not concern themselves about any thing else, for their attentions were devoted to a huge kettle placed upon a blazing fire, the contents of which they kept continually stirring. A great deal of baggage was strewed around the tents, and the mules were huddled together in packs, on the outside of these temporary habitations. The smoke of cigars was liberally distributed on all sides; and as they reclined near the fires in loud converse and raillery, they strongly resembled a desperate horde of robbers at their evening carousal. My appearance checked for a moment their mirth, and as I passed through the busy file, we exchanged a great many *vivas!* but I must confess I was not sorry to leave them as fast as possible. I reached Santos without further interruption.

The streets of this town of an evening have a dark and lonely aspect, for the corners of them are not embellished with a smiling and illuminated Virgin. The grog shops were full of Brazilian, American, and English sailors, the latter possibly stragglers from ships at Rio, who had been detained when on shore on leave, made drunk, and afterwards kidnapped on board some of the Brazilian men-of-war, a method a good deal practised at Rio by a desperate set of fellows who received a certain gratuity for every sailor thus entrapped: the Beagle lost a number of men in this manner. Some of these sailors become worthless and drunken characters, and are infinitely worse to meet in the streets of a night than the natives themselves. They are a begging and abusive set, and frequently get into rows with the tawny militia, the effects of which are visible on the faces of both parties in the morning. On proceeding to the beach, in the hope of getting off to the ship, I found every canoe hauled up, and I then made the best of my way to a house of accommodation in the vicinity, the best the town afforded, and kept by an ancient mulatto woman, who had been introduced to my notice by Mr. Kilkenny. The lady welcomed me with much cordiality, and guessing by my look that I needed both refreshment and rest, she stirred with her foot a sullen and awkward negress, who was fast asleep upon a mat in the corner of the room, and who raised herself slowly up nearly in the same state as Venus when she first arose firom the sea, but not with the attractions of the Venus Corregio has painted so exquisitely—the lovely limbs kissing the transparent water—but more resembling the Hottentot beauty some years since imported into this admiring country. The table was soon spread out, and decorated with *gallinhas* (fowls) and other eatables, and a choice of wines and spirits. While I supped, the good hostess asked me many questions about St. Paulo (for she had never been out of Santos), all of which I answered with brevity, but with great fidelity; but as I perceived she was bent upon hearing the whole particulars, I related all the incidents of the journey. However, frequently during the recital, I was much surprised, and somewhat piqued, to see this tawny listener rubbing her hands in a sort of ecstasy, and exclaim "*Filho de puta Inglese,*" and I took occasion, looking serious, to explain to her that such words were not at all to my taste. Whereupon she told me what, until then, I had no idea of—that when a Brazilian is delighted with any person, those words are used as a compliment—a piece of information I afterwards ascertained to be correct. The hostess, taking the hint, by my eyes involuntarily closing, that I had remained up long enough, acted accordingly, and ordered the old negress to show me my bed-room, who led the way to a neat furnished apartment on the ground-floor, and there placing the candle on the table, silently withdrew, casting at me a very singular look as she shut the door. As the room was small and confined, I opened the window, which looked out upon a garden, where orange-trees and flowers perfumed the air; but I did not remain long to enjoy the fragrance, for overcome by fatigue, I threw myself on the couch, and, in spite of a formidable attack of mosquitos, soon fell into a deep sleep. But I did not long enjoy it, for I was awoke by finding myself encircled in the arms of the old negress who had conducted me to my chamber, and who, unhappily for me, had found her way in through the window: had she been twenty years younger, I possibly might have thanked her for her courtesy. In the morning I hastened on board, where I learnt that a ball had been given by a rich inhabitant, to which our officers had been invited. I wished that I had been there, having a great desire to see the manner in which the Brazilians at Santos conducted this amusement, of which they are passionately fond; neither did I wait long for an opportunity, for fortune introduced me, quite unexpectedly, to a dance the very next evening. On my entrance, I beheld a pleasing sight, for in the centre of a large room a number of buxom senhoras and gallant senhors were capering away to the sound of fiddles and violincellos. As it was pleasant enough to observe them, without taking a share in the bustle, I soon made my way towards the master of the Beagle, whom I saw seated next to as good-natured a lady as ever peeled a banana. With this lady he seemed highly pleased; but he could not help expressing his uneasiness at her superior method of speaking Portuguese, yet, as she condescendingly used the words *si, si,* to most of his questions, there could be little doubt but she understood all Mr. Flinn said to her. After the dancers had engaged in a sort of waltz, in which was displayed a great many difficult steps and figures, they all retired to their places, and I observed some others of the party employed in coaxing a little fat figure of a lady to dance, which she declined; but her excuses were over-ruled by a great majority, and she advanced to the middle of the room, attended by a person whom I easily recognised to be the commandant who had boarded us in the river. When they had gone through a few preliminary and grotesque movements, to the great delight of the whole company, they began their dance. As I have witnessed the bolero, this dance reminded me of it, only very drolly burlesqued; and although I have seen it executed by other persons at Rio, after some very awkward efforts, yet the couple before me behaved with much ardour and spirit. The lady, in particular, was quite *degagée*, and threw into the performance as much wriggle of body and snapping of fingers as was requisite to give effect, and occasion the laughter of the delighted observers, for in spite of her being "a dumpy woman," she possessed a considerable share of *badin*; and was decidedly the best dancer in the room. It was impossible to be fatigued with this society, for there was not a sad countenance among them; in short, every performance of the above description seemed to excite their good-humour, and made each person anxious to display his talent in this favourite dance; indeed, the Brazilians take great delight in this pastime, during which they are extremely vivacious. It was my fortune, however, this night to be a spectator of a dance of another description, and executed by a different company, for near twelve o'clock I had, attracted by the serenity of the evening, wandered from the ball-room to an open space near the outlets of the town, where I beheld, before a miserable shed, a number of negros and negresses standing together in a circle. I seemed to have arrived very apropos, for they were just commencing the dance of their country: for the benefit of the air and this diversion, I seated myself near them, and awaited patiently their circumrotatory amusement. For some minutes they behaved very rationally; however, the oddities that marked their character soon became manifest, for one of the throng (a female) appeared in the centre of the sombre ring, having her clothes bundled about her person, to give a greater freedom to her limbs, which were bare from the knee downwards, and commenced such lively capers, wriggles, and flings, that "Nannie," of Kirk Alloway notoriety would have been a mere *figurante* by the side of her. During her exertions the rest of her people remained stationary, clapping their hands and looking wistfully around as they uttered low noises. I could not discover whether my presence had any effect upon their movements, but when this Venus had finished she returned to her place, and another limber and active negress leaped forward, suitably equipped, and fully equalled the former in the variety as well as vigour of her *coupés*. When this person had sufficiently distinguished herself, she also retired, and her place was supplied by a tall, raw-boned negro, who, not content with dealing out (as he jumped about the circle) some heavy thumps on the heads of his comrades, but he also carried the freak so far as to kick up his foot so close to their faces, that had either of them possessed a nose like a "pudding's end," they would have received a formidable "upcut," but happily for them their noses were compressed flat to their faces, and consequently escaped the shock. By the time this gaunt black had worked himself up to a pitch of frenzy, he was joined by another, who danced into the ring, and these two persons exchanged civilities by slapping each other on the face with great fervour. But this mania, in a short time, extended to the rest, for they began to pummel one another in a manner which, to me, appeared a great deal more like earnest than fun; and I was not long in doubt, for the women, as well as the men, seized each other by the woolly skull, and bestowed so many unruly knocks there, that the blood streamed from their dilated nostrils; and during this noisy conflict they all swore in good Portuguese, and their heads frequently came in contact, and rattled like pins in a skittle-ground. As there was no unfair advantage taken on either side, I did not believe I had any right to interfere, and I therefore remained very quiet, wondering how this midnight brawl would end, when suddenly a heavy tramp was heard approaching, accompanied by a clang of arms. In a moment they had ceased fighting, and all were seen to scamper in various directions, for a party of the police arrived, and succeeded in lodging some of them in gaol. I was told by the Guard, that instances had been known, during these dances, of quarrels ensuing, in which they have fought with knives most furiously, and that to prevent these combats they are obliged to bestow upon the offenders a liberal allowance of *pao* (stick), which, like the bamboo of the Chinese, has a marvellous power in keeping them in awe.

A wealthy Brazilian in Santos had been long ill: he applied to Captain Stokes, who requested our assistant-surgeon to visit him. In a few days the *malade* (such was the beneficial result of Mr. Bynoe's attendance) was able to lay aside his crutches, and dismiss his nurse. The fame of this disciple of Hippocrates soon spread in the town, and an offer was made to him to leave the service and settle among them—a certain salary being guaranteed by a person of some note in the place. This proposition Mr. Bynoe thought fit to refuse; and as he also declined all pecuniary remuneration, we were surprised one morning by a canoe coming alongside, in which was a black slave with a large basket upon his head, covered with a white napkin. He was the bearer of a present from the recovered Brazilian to the doctor, which consisted of some bottles of wine and lengthy sponge cakes, of excellent flavour, besides a number of sweetmeats. This was a very agreeable relish, for we were all fond of "sweeties," and at Santos it went hard with us, for there was no pastrycook in the town. Our carpenter, too, had an offer of employment in the dockyard at good pay, but he, likewise, was averse to leave his "pound and pint" for any sinecure under this same government.

There used to come daily alongside the ship a canoe furnished with bread, milk, fruit, and many other provisions, for the convenience of the ship's company (if they chose to purchase). One morning our steward was absent, and having occasion for a variety of eatables, we asked a diminutive seaman named Lewis (who, when dressed in his blanket-jacket and trousers, had the appearance of a small white bear of Greenland) to fetch certain provisions from the canoe. As we sat in the berth, waiting his arrival, we were surprised to see a quantity of butter (which in this climate is not very firm) come spank down upon the deck, and spread out like a pancake. This singular descent was followed by a rare shower of eggs, bananas, oranges, and small loaves, and last, not least, little Lewis rolled down head over heels, and lay amidst his purchase in a most graceless situation. Upon inquiring into the cause of this singular behaviour he informed us that he had filled his arms too full, and as he descended the ladder at the main hatch, keeping every thing steady with his chin, he heard the direful smack occasioned by the escape of the butter, which so unnerved him, that in his confusion he let fall the eggs and the rest of the provisions, and missing his footstep he came down after them, most unwillingly, in the manner described.

I sometimes met on shore (at the hotel kept by the mulatto woman) a tall, distracted-looking Yankee: whenever he saw me, he would always introduce himself by a "How d'ye do, sir; I intend, sir, to come on board, and visit your rooms" (meaning the berth). As he was known to some of the officers on board, I said we should be glad to see him; but this day he annoyed me very much by telling me about the Americans, and wished to enter into a dispute respecting their navy and our own, which I thought ill-timed, there being some strangers present, but when he asked me what I thought of the Americans, I replied "that I never thought about them at all." This speech, I afterwards understood, offended him for life. The next day he came on board, and towards evening he visited "our rooms," when we regaled him with egg flip, and not being disposed to go on shore, he was accommodated with one of our hammocks. I have a habit of laughing in my sleep (although I sometimes groan, as my messmates well know), upon which the Yankee put a very singular construction, for the next morning, when I came into the berth, he said, "How d'ye do, sir; I calculate you get some gold-dust at St. Paulo, I do." "What makes you think so?" "I guess you laugh in your sleep."

In a few days Captain Stokes returned from St. Paulo, after having visited the gold mines and the cathedral, where Lieutenant Sholl, being incommoded by his large straw hat, was seen very deliberately to roll it up and put it in his coat-pocket. This mode of disposing of his straw hat was observed by some of the young ladies near him, and they could not resist breaking out into a titter at the novelty, but their mirth was further excited when, on leaving the church, Lieutenant Sholl had occasion to put the hat upon his head, for it was by no means in its original shape, and required some coaxing to look "as well as ever." I began to be tired of remaining at this anchorage, although when on shore I made shift to amuse myself; but there were two things which surprised me very much, the first was that no skyrockets or other fireworks were exhibited during our stay, and the second that the "chanticleers" of Santos crow with a very shrill note, which is prolonged for nearly half a minute. There was a little rough feathered bantam, that used to peck near the beach, who would stretch out his neck and crow for such an unusual time, as often to occasion a laugh among the sailors on board. Mr. Whittaker having occasion to visit Paranagua (our next destination) he came on board, and we left Santos town on the 3d of July, and very soon cleared the river, and put to sea with a fair wind. The Pampero had sailed to convoy a number of small craft, bound to the island of St. Catherine, for this part of the coast was infested by a Buenos Ayrian privateer, who frequently "practised as a sea attorney," to the great detriment of the Brazilians. We had left the harbour but a few hours when it fell stark calm, and such numbers of petrels and other sea birds hovered in the wake of the ship that we amused ourselves by catching them, which was accomplished by baiting small fish-hooks with a piece of fat beef, and casting them on the water. The birds were all eager for the dainty morsel, and such as were successful in seizing the bait we hauled on board. The most curiously feathered we preserved as specimens, all others were set at liberty, unless prevented by their having taken too powerful a gorge, which required the hook being cut out. The weather continuing fine, the men were exercised at quarters, at which they had become very expert, but ere we were two days old at sea (as Hamlet says) we saw a sail to windward, and we presently observed she was in chace of us. This stranger could not have come down in better time, for our guns were loaded with round and canister, and the men, being exercised, were armed with cutlass and pistols, and by the time she came within hail every man was at his station. She was a large fine brig, and now hoisted Buenos Ayrian colours, and we immediately run up the English flag, whereupon the privateer fired a gun to windward, and neared us amazingly fast. As the ship ran down under our stern, Captain Stokes, who was on the poop, surveyed them very cooly and answered their hail, and Mr. Whittaker took this opportunity to go below and pull off his summer jacket and put on his uniform coat. The Buenos Ayrian having come close to us on the larboard bow, I observed that her deck was literally crowded with men, but she carried few guns, and had a famous long Tom in midships. Altogether she looked as if she meant nothing but fighting, and cut a most formidable appearance.

"Who would not brave the battle fire, the wreck,
To move the monarch of her peopled deck."

The privateer sent her boat on board with two officers, one of whom informed Captain Stokes that the brig was the General Brandzen Buenos Ayrian Privateer, commanded by an American named Haidey, and that a day or two previous they had fallen in with a Brazilian twenty-gun ship and a schooner. The ship had sailed off very fast, and left the schooner to fight; but they had taken her after a slight resistance; and having sent on board the captured vessel an officer and some men from the privateer, she had sailed for Buenos Ayres. The commander and chief officer of the schooner were Frenchmen; and then prisoners on board the General Brandzen, but Captain Haidey was desirous of landing them on the Coast of Brazil (having given to each a certificate of their courage in defending the schooner), and hearing that we were bound to Paranagua, he requested to know if Captain Stokes was willing to receive them on board and land then at that place. I need not acquaint my reader that Captain Stokes acceded to take the vanquished Frenchmen on board; and while he held some further conversation with the chief officer, the other (who had a cutlass by his side of a most formidable appearance) asked me if I had seen anything of the Pampero. I told him that she had just sailed from Santos towards St. Catherines, and I was about to give an account of the small craft when I was prevented by Mr. Kirke, who cautioned me to keep quiet, and took an opportunity of telling me that we had no right to give them any information—a circumstance I had quite overlooked, but which was certainly very true. The boat now rowed off to the privateer, and in a short time returned with the two Frenchmen and their baggage, and these gentlemen having come on board, the officers of the privateer bid us adieu, saying as they went over the side, " Now for the Pampero." The General Brandzen did not keep us company a long time, for a breeze springing up, she crowded all sail, and was soon out of sight, to the great joy of the Frenchmen, who were very happy at finding themselves (so unexpectedly) on board the Beagle.

The commander of the schooner had been some time in the service of the Emperor of

Brazil, and was generally very fortunate in eluding this sort of privateers, to which he had a particular aversion, but it was his ill-luck to sail in company with the twenty-gun ship and to be taken. Had the crew of the schooner behaved in any way like men, and given one good broadside for the honour of the Emperor of Brazil, that would have been something to boast of, but no sooner did the canister shot from the privateer rattle among the schooner's men, than they all fell flat on their faces upon the deck, to the great astonishment of the two Frenchmen, who were obliged to fire the guns themselves; and it was no easy matter to rouse these mulatto sailors up again, and not before they were boarded by the privateer did they come to their senses. What we are to think of the twenty-gun ship is another affair; perhaps her commander discovered that the only method of coming off victorious was by running away.

On a Sunday, when the weather permitted, prayers were read to the ship's company, who came aft and seated themselves on the quarter-deck—the gentleman who officiated as clergyman standing at the capstan. We had on board a number of small pigs, and one morning just as the service commenced, one of the animals escaped from under the forecastle, and made its way aft, with sundry little frisks and jumps. Upon the first appearance of the "*petit cochon*" all eyes were naturally fixed upon the visitor, who stood as if listening to the doctrine (a learned pig), but occasionally interrupted the speaker by a playful squeal and grunt. This annoyance, and the other pigs endeavouring likewise to escape being very clamorous, caused a break off in the service much in the following manner:—"Dearly beloved brethren, the Scripture moveth us in sundry places to (quarter master, take away this pig) acknowledge and confess our manifold sins and (silence those pigs, forward) and that we should not dissemble nor cloak them before (that will do, that will do,)"——. But this was not the only interruption, for a little Santos cock, which had been brought on board, would crow with such a long dismal note as to occasion something like a smile to circulate from face to face.

As we neared the land a dense fog set in, and it was a long while before we could venture to cross the bar of Paranagua; but falling in with a fishing-boat, the master of her undertook to pilot us to the town; but in consequence of the thick fogs, we did not anchor off the Ilha de Cotingo until the 9th of July. Upon the extreme end of this land there was a large white cross erected, for some distinguishing land-mark, but the town of Paranagua is nearly two miles further, and as there would have been some difficulty in getting the Beagle up to the town, we remained here until we again weighed anchor.

This island, in many places, is exceedingly steep and woody, and alongshore we observed a few ill-constructed wooden huts, which were built half a mile from each other. The next day, the weather being delightfully warm and fine, I was solicitous to get on shore, and accompanied the assistant-surgeon on a shooting excursion, when both of us being landed near the cross, we scrambled along the slippery rocks which skirt the beach, and arrived at one of the poor-looking huts. We here found a family;

consisting of a lame old man (a native of Pico) and two pretty young women (his daughters), also a young fisherman, who had married the eldest of the girls. It was scarcely possible to refrain from laughter at the whimsical reception given us by these good-tempered creatures, for as we came near them, they all huddled together, and thrust the old man foremost, who leant upon his stick and grinned very facetiously, while a little boy, son to the fisherman, peeped at us from behind a large excrescence which grew from the old man's hip. The fisherman had just returned from casting his nets, and going into the hut he brought out a basket filled with large fish of different descriptions, and abundance of prawns as large as small lobsters, and selecting some of the finest fish from the basket, he offered to dress them for our repast, a proposition to which we readily agreed. Having thus established some sort of entertainment, we betook ourselves to the mountains, and coming to a banana plantation, we shot two or three humming-birds, although in one instance I was so fortunate as to miss the bird and knock down a banana tree. We also shot some small parrots, and having knocked the feathers out of the turkey buzzards, which soar near the top of the mountains, we returned, and found the young ladies busily employed in looking into the fish-kettle, and some knives and forks were laid upon a table, without a cloth, placed under the shade of some orange trees near the house. I could not avoid feeling great pleasure at this sight, and while dinner was being served up the old man told us that he had lived on this spot nearly forty years, during which he had fared very badly, and for the last ten years neither himself nor family had tasted fresh meat above a dozen times. Their general food was dried beef, fresh and salt fish, prawns, and the farina served them for bread, which they very seldom tasted. All these privations gave him little uneasiness, but his hip teazed him very much, and he was very solicitous to know if our surgeon could devise some method of cure. Upon Mr. Bynoe telling him it was quite hopeless, he fetched from the hut much such another small house as Mr. Simon Paap (the dwarf) used to be confined in at the fairs, and having opened the door we perceived in the inside a sleek and comely St. Antonio surrounded by relics—pictures of saints and small waxen Madonnas. After we had made an offering of a few pieces to the jolly saint, the old man shut the box and returned with it into the house.

The females had tamed a number of small parrots, which flew about the orange trees, and frequently came and perched upon their shoulders; and many other small birds, of beautiful plumage, were confined in cages depending from the different trees. Before we departed, the ladies expressed a wish for some ship's beef and biscuits, a taste we determined to gratify, and the next day we brought on shore a small basket of such provisions as our mess afforded, with a few bottles of wine and a magnum of rare Hollands. We could also have furnished them with some shoes and stockings, but these comforts would have been quite superfluous, for all the inhabitants we saw upon this island, men, women, and children, ran about barefooted, fearless of snakes which here abound, but in spite of this exposure they are seldom or ever bitten. Having disposed of the basket, we proceeded to the uplands, and met with much the same success as on the former day; but on our return to the hut we were not a little surprised to find that our friends had given an entertainment to their neighbours, for several persons were convened at the hut, who had been ingenious enough to empty some of the wine bottles, but there had been a general combination in favour of the Hollands, which was all drunk. I verily believe they had not been so happy for some time: the old man was twenty years younger, and would have danced but for the pain in his hip. The Hollands had made him so very social and elated that he began to throw out hints of our settling among them, and I must add (vanity apart), that one of us had an offer of marriage with the younger daughter, a lively, airy nymph of seventeen.

The next day Mr. Bynoe went to the town of Paranagua, where he had been requested to go in order to visit some of the afflicted inhabitants (for they had no resident surgeon), who were suffering at this time from the visitation of a wandering quack, who had made sad havoc among them, and distributed daily a number of red pills, which he pronounced to be a panacea in all disorders. An old padre, who ought to have known better, had placed such firm reliance upon the virtue of these pills in curing him of syphilis, that he was reduced in a short time to the deplorable condition of poor Pangloss— "every time he attempted to spit, out dropt a tooth." There were some others who had suffered from the calamities of the red pills, and this famous practitioner was blessed with a becoming assurance, which carried him through the country; and doubtless all those who underwent the ceremony of bolting these aforesaid pills had no cause to hug themselves upon their good fortune. Most of the people at Paranagua entertained a suspicion that we were pirates, nor could they, for some time, be persuaded to the contrary. There are as many padres, saints, and sinners as need be in such a small town, and the natives seem little disposed to improve their condition by trade or agriculture, for the greater part of them are indolent, and do little else than smoke cigars, sprinkle holy water, and suck *matté*. The adjacent lands are but thinly inhabited, and such as exist there support themselves by fishing. We heard of an Englishman who had a good establishment somewhere on the banks of the river, and he was reported to be a good, hospitable fellow, particularly to his countrymen, or indeed to any who stood in need of his assistance.

The temperature is delightful in spite of the heavy fogs, which, however, do not last long, and the climate is very favourable to an European constitution. The inhabitants are generally healthy and long-lived. The fisherman at the hut sometimes came alongside in his canoe, and brought off for sale a number of roes of fish, dried and salted, and dried prawns, both which made excellent additions to the breakfast-table; but Mr. Nobody (a troublesome fellow in a ship) would sometimes enter our berth in the night, and carry off a considerable quantity of this sea-stock, together with rum, and whatever he could lay his hands on. One night, however,

Mr. Nobody was found crawling out, well laden, upon his hands and knees, but upon his promising faithfully never to visit us again, we let him off, to his unspeakable satisfaction. He kept his promise, and never came again. Mr. Whittaker and the two Frenchmen had left the ship, and were preparing to return to Santos overland, by no means, I was given to understand, a pleasant way of travelling about this part of the coast, for the roads are excessively bad, and the journey one of much trouble and fatigue.

Early on the morning of our departure from this anchorage, which was on the 12th of July, we missed from the ship a marine and a second class boy, and our steward, not being longer disposed to make puddings or clean knives, " nor scrape trenchering, nor wash dish," had accompanied them, not forgetting to take with him a quantity of biscuits and cheese. They had escaped in the first gig, which lay alongside, and rowed round the point, and there landed and made her fast. These persons intended, doubtless, to vegetate with the old man and his family, for I rather believe our steward had overheard our praises, particularly of Donna Marguerita and Donna Rosa, whom we represented as a prodigy of beauty. Every search was made for these stragglers, at the hut and about the grounds, but without success, and we were obliged to sail without them. On towing outwards, towards the entrance of the river, near the dusk of the evening, a clear and loud report of fire-arms was distinguished, supposed to proceed from a Swedish brig, which was lying here when we came in, then at anchor a league a-head of us. On its continuance, the captain ordered the gig to be manned (each seaman armed with a cutlass and pistol), and Lieutenant Sholl and a midshipman were sent to ascertain the cause, we all conjecturing that some mutiny or riotous conduct had taken place on board the Swede. As the gig neared the brig, the firing became more rapid, and a faint halloo was borne along the water; whereupon Captain Stokes made for the brig, also, in the cutter, well armed. The gig soon returned, with an account that the Swedish captain and all on board were considerably drunk, for having that day received a visit from the governor of Paranagua, the Swede had chosen the stillness of evening to celebrate the honour done him, and had kept up a regular exercise of guns and small arms. His mate, I rather believe an Englishman, was civil, but his commander was altogether gloriously in the wind, and much inclined to disapprove of our coming on board, by his observing, as the officers entered the gangway, "It is ver strange dat von poor Swede cannot amuse himself vid-out von Englishman coming to interrupt him;" then turning to his mate he said, "Mr. Veb, fire two more gun immediately." Lieutenant Sholl left him hiccupping about the deck, endeavouring to eructate his invectives against our ship's crew, but in vain—potent *aquadente* had rendered him nearly speechless. The next morning we anchored alongside the Swede, and so obscure a fog set in, that we could not see five paces before us; the wind died away, and the weather proved so disgraceful and hazy, that we began to get out of humour. The black cook took this opportunity to be even with one of the marines (who had a bad cough) for stealing his "varm vater" from the coppers, for he crammed the fire full of green wood, which sent forth a thick black smoke that affected the eyes very much. This smoke, combined with the fog, soon pervaded the lower deck, and tickling the lungs of the marine, brought on such a fit of coughing, that, to prevent being choked, he was obliged to stagger upon deck. The success of this trick caused the black to laugh and giggle with delight, and as he busied himself about the fire, he was heard to exclaim, "Dam tief, I larn you steal my varm vater for shave." The captain of the Swede, in spite of the fog, found his way on board the Beagle, and apologized for the ill manners of the preceding evening. He was bound to Valparaiso with a cargo of *matté*, for which, at the town of Paranagua, he had paid at the rate of two dollars per pound, but at Valparaiso he expected to realise upwards of twenty dollars per pound. He represented most of the Brazilians at the town as indolent, and not at all inclined to encourage him in bringing stores. Agricultural instruments were in great request, but not one would undertake to buy a certain quantity if he should bring out any, and he did not think it advisable to take such a cargo, unless he was certain of selling it. They have no spirit for trade.

On the 16th of July we got under weigh, with an intention of passing the bar, having a pilot on board (Domingo Antonio); but another thick fog set in, and compelled us to anchor until it had passed. We again weighed, and again a fog brought us up near the Ilha dos Palmos (Palm Island). When off the fort upon the Island of Mêle they hailed us to ask where we were bound, and wishing us a *bom viage;* by half past three we had cleared the river and all difficulty of repassing the bar, and stood away towards St. Catherine's, the weather fine "and happy breezes blew."

On the 18th of July we made the land, and anchored off Fort Santa Cruz, but as we entered the harbour we were saluted by the Pampero with seventeen guns, which we returned. There was a French frigate, La Durance, also lying in the roads, bound to the Island of Bourbon with a detachment of artillery, and had put in for wood and water, having been two months on her passage from Brest. The captain and first lieutenant of the Pampero came on board the Beagle, and were invited to dine with Captain Stokes, who did not fail to acquaint them of the friendly inquiries made by the Buenos Ayrian, but this communication did not give them much uneasiness.

On the 19th, I accompanied Mr. Kirke and Mr. Bynoe upon a shooting excursion to the main land, but finding the path we had chosen led to a few straggling houses at the back of Fort Santa Cruz, we retraced our steps through the woods, catching an occasional glance of the gaudy toucan, with its large beak, as it flew among the trees. We heard some strange gobbling noises in the deep jungles, which we were afterwards told proceeded from wild turkeys, and we began to hope that chance would bring us within range of these noisy birds, and also of the parroquets, which often flew over our heads with a screaming note, but at too great a height to be brought down. In a certain part of this wood we struck off into another obscure path, which we found led towards a remote part of the sea-shore, where the shrill scream of the sea-gull strikes upon the ear, and the continual whirling and shrieking these birds keep up over your head, make you often inclined to fire at them to get rid of the annoyance. Pursuing another path, which skirted the base of a mountain, we came to some cottages, which we found pre-occupied by a party of French artillerymen, and one of them was in loud contention with the master of the cottage (a Brazilian) respecting the settlement for aquedente and other liquors, which he had supplied for their refreshment.

Senhor Brazellero did not understand French, and he accordingly blazed away in Portuguese, and twanged off the *nao antiende* with great ferocity, to the visible chagrin of *pauvre Jean Francois*, who not being able to speak Portuguese, poured in a broadside of French slang, and *f—tre*, *Diable*, and *sacre*, with a suitable gesture, was repeatedly uttered. During this uproar one of the Frenchman's companions (a raw-boned, hard-fisted fellow) suddenly seized the Brazilian by the chin, which he pinched and shook with such a hearty good will that the poor senhor roared with anguish. After this strange behaviour the Frenchmen very quickly left the house, and they had no sooner disappeared than the Brazilian ran about the room in a very frantic condition, and almost cried with vexation. But during this paroxysm he drew forth a large carving knife, and practised before us the way that he would serve the Frenchman, for he darted out his arm as if to catch him by the throat, and made several severe stabs; he then appeared to throw the body upon the ground, while he stood over it with a vengeful look, like the Giaour over the fallen Hassan. We had some difficulty in preventing him rushing out of the house in search of the Frenchman, and had Maître Jean returned during the performance, he certainly would have been spitted by the long knife of the infuriated Brazilian. When he became a little calm he ventured to introduce us to his wives (for he was so happy as to have two), who were young, thick-lipped negresses of irresistible charms, and a numerous family of tawny children were scudding about the plantations; but these skipping nudities, I observed, frequently stood still and scratched their heads with both hands, and this clawing appeared to give them great ease and satisfaction.

In traversing the mountains which lay at the further end of the grounds, I shot a brown bird, about the size of a pigeon, but it had a tail a foot and a half in length, of long straight feathers. As we returned back we met the Brazilian, and I asked him the name of the bird, which he said was an *alma de gata* (soul of a cat), and he appeared to have a great antipathy to this kind of bird, and was very glad that I had shot one. In expectation of meeting with some wild turkeys, I had put a good charge in the gun, and as he wished to try his skill in shooting at a mark, I gave him the fowling piece to discharge. After taking aim for five minutes, he pulled the trigger, and the gun flew out of his hands, having first given him such a knock on the jaw, and bruised his Brazilian shoulder, that he was not the least desirous of another shot. On the following day I was on shore with Mr. Bynoe, and towards evening we came to a well-built house, the owner of which was an Englishman, who had resided there many years. He was greatly rejoiced at meeting with his countrymen, and gave us a hearty welcome, and we were presently introduced to his wife and daughters, natives of St. Catherine's, who were employed in making flowers of some small shells, fastened upon wire and decorated with silver. We were about to proceed onwards to the beach, when he begged of us to stay, and he would make it a night of rejoicing; we were fearful of exceeding our leave, but upon his promising to take us off in his canoe as soon as the morning dawned, we consented to remain. Meanwhile the wife and daughters set about making tankards of egg-flip and bowls of milk punch, and appeared much pleased by our taking a plentiful libation of both. It appeared that they had sent into the neighbourhood for some other ladies, for several senhoras of soft and sleek-looking persons soon arrived, and a room being cleared for dancing, English Jack, for such was he called by the Portuguese, stuck himself in a corner of the room, with an old fife,

> "And hotch'd and blew wi' might and main;"

while all of us skipped about with surprising agility and perseverance; and this agreeable amusement continued with great obstinacy until past three o'clock in the morning, by which time the ladies, seeming disposed to sleep, retired to their homes, and the dancing ended. In all probability we should not have awakened very early, had we not been disturbed by our host, who came to tell us that his canoe, upon trial, was too leaky for service, and that it would be two hours before he could get her in readiness, or even borrow one from his neighbours, who were all out fishing. Upon this intimation it was decided that we should go to the mountain and pass the time in shooting, in which recreation we found means to beguile our time very pleasantly, being decoyed up the mountain, by the sight of numberless birds, much further than we intended. This sport, favourable as it was, did not make us forget the ship, for, on arriving at a part of the mountain which commanded a view of St. Catherine's Bay, we looked out for the Beagle, and were surprised to perceive her sails unfurled, and four guns fired in succession. Being convinced that this was a signal for us to come off, we did not choose our path down, but in our hurry stumbled over every impediment, and I was so happy as to select a passage over some fimbers which had been burnt down, and this mistake made me appear as if I had descended a chimney. The instant we arrived on the beach we launched the canoe, for the leak had been in some degree stopped, and English Jack and his son hoisted sail and managed the boat while we baled out the water with our hats, and in this manner we arrived alongside about twelve o'clock. We had just time to make our host amends for his entertainment, when he was ordered to shove off, the hands being piped on deck, having first tucked into his hat one half of a plum-pudding, which had just left the coppers, and smoked upon the table in our berth.

On the 21st of July we stood out to sea with a fair wind, but it suddenly chopped round, and blew directly in our teeth with great fury, which towards night increased to a hurricane. This weather continued all the 23d and 24th, during which we were exposed to a very heavy sea, which hurled the vessel along, almost mocking the skill and calculations of the captain; and during the continuance of the gale we shipped so many seas, and the vessel laboured so much, that some few on board were sea-sick; and the clerk was a rare fellow for the nausea, inasmuch that whenever he was asked to dine with the gun-room officers, he generally preferred accepting their invitation in fair weather. These gales of wind are frequently accompanied by thunder and lightning; the atmosphere becomes dark as night, and the skimming of the stormy petrels round the ship, seem, by their rapid flight, to be aware of the approaching storm. The sea appears lashed into a foam, and the lightning darting through the heavens in twenty different forms, sometimes descends, dreadfully forked, into the sea, close alongside the ship: the loud and heavy peals of thunder, and the dashing of the spray over the vessel as she ploughs her way through the water, present altogether such an awful sight, that all those who "live at home at ease" can have little idea of.

On the 5th of August we came into Monte Video, having been a fortnight on a passage which is usually made in three days. We found all of them (as usual) in Monte Video very anxious about getting money, and the gazelle-eyed senhoras as much on the *qui vive* as ever, for several of these ladies had been married to Brazilian officers. About the 10th of the month we again put to sea, and in our passage back to Rio we called in at Santos, where we heard that Mr. Whittaker had arrived overland from Paranagua, and that the Frenchmen had proceeded to Rio Janeiro *via* St. Paulo. On the following day we sailed from this harbour, and arrived in a short time at Rio Janeiro. After we had been here some time, the Adventure sailed for Santos and Monte Video, where the

Beagle was to join her, preparatory to our final departure for the Straits of Magellan. I had forgot to mention, that before the departure of that ship, the clerk of her was on shore with the assistant-surgeon of the Beagle, and as they were walking leisurely along in the cool of the evening, Mr. Bynoe suddenly felt across his head and shoulders a number of lusty thwacks with a cudgel. At this rude salutation he turned hastily round, and perceived three or four negroes scampering away in great haste, who were immediately pursued by the clerk; but the negroes were well acquainted with the localities of the place, and soon eluded pursuit. Thus did the brawny slaves escape, who, doubtless, had been tutored and set on by their master, for some imaginary and jealous suspicion, to perform such an assassin-like act. Nor was this the only instance, for a few evenings afterwards a mate from one of our ships was assaulted by a party of negroes, and would have had his skull fractured, had it not been for the goodness of a glazed cocked hat, which, however, was cut through with a bludgeon.

Being on shore one day with Mr. Bynoe, chance directed us to the convent of San Francisco de Paulo, and feeling disposed to amuse ourselves, we entered the church, in order to take a review of the images, saints, and relics, which are here harboured in great plenty. We had not been here many minutes, before we observed a huge padre enter the building, and disappear through a door in a corner of the aisle. Wishing to ascertain where the door led, we determined to follow the footsteps of the pious man, and both of us quickly vanished through the partition, which we found conducted to a small square attached to the convent, where a number of fat and chubby padres were waddling about, with great ease and devotion, at the further end of a paved alley. As we had entered "merely out of curiosity," we deemed it no harm to walk about on the other side, and contemplate the numerous *nossa senhoras* placed in the niches of the wall, and defended by a net-work of iron. Presently we heard a great rustling of garments, and on looking round we perceived the whole bevy of monks charging us with great ferocity, their long and heavy rosaries clattering by their sides as they bounced along. When they came near enough, one of the friars, more blowsy and querulous than the rest, pointed to our hats, which unfortunately we had neglected to remove from our heads, and motioned us to take them off. Having complied with this request, for this was a very holy place, I asked him if he could speak French; but he said he only spoke Latin and Portuguese, and I attempted a few school phrases in the Latin tongue, but he answered me with a very surly "*non entiende,*" and his Portuguese appeared to me a sort of *lingua Franca* not over intelligible. By this time our curiosity had begun to abate, and as we were honoured by their attendance wherever we moved, I readily guessed they were not at all pleased at our stay; but not wishing to give these honest people any further uneasiness, we walked towards the door, several of them giving us some very significant grins as we departed. In crossing the Rua d'Ouvidor we met a string of felons, driven (as usual) by a grim mulatto soldier, and one of the negroes seemed rather willing to loiter by the way. This inclination being perceived by the mulatto driver, who had a drawn cutlass in his hand, he gave the black several severe blows with the flat part of it; but the edge of the blade sometimes came in contact with the bare shoulders of the slave, and sliced him so severely, that the blood trickled down his arms, and made the rest of the party rush quickly forward with very gloomy faces. The slaves very frequently supply the place of horses, for the most laborious work is done by the negroes; and often have I seen a number of these, almost naked wretches, tottering along the Rua Dereita, scarcely able to sustain the heavy burdens which they are doomed to carry, and as they hurry along, their dark skins shining with perspiration, they break out into strange and mournful noises, or rather a wild kind of native song; and this melody seems to cheer them up and lighten their heavy task. It is well known in Rio that some of the Portuguese send their slaves out to beg in the streets (all who have remained at this city must often have been asked for a vintim by some of the negro boys or men), and if they should not bring home a certain sum, they catch *pao;* but to avoid this unwelcome salutation, they are very industrious in begging, and there is also another stimulus, for all the money collected above the specified amount is their own.

I scarcely ever observed the shop of a negro barber that had not a large ram's horn nailed up on the inside, as a preventive against all magic and infernal influence, for they are very superstitious; neither could I induce any of them to sell this Obi charm, for I have frequently offered them money to take it down, but without success. These crooked horns (without the Obi, which is furnished by some of the old negro women,) are sometimes carried about for sale in the streets, the sharp end daubed with red paint.

The atmosphere is sometimes very heavy and oppressive, and frequently of a night the rain descends with such violence as to inundate the streets in a short time. When this is the case, the lower Portuguese take off their shoes and stockings and walk home bare legged, and a number of blacks station themselves at the corner of the different streets in order to earn a few vintims by carrying on their shoulders any person desirous of crossing. But they are not always to be trusted, for I have seen them, when they supported a weighty Brazellero, suddenly stumble and pitch their unwelcome load into the muddy stream. After this feat (when the person has gone) they grin with delight, and their extravagant gestures prove how much they enjoy this sort of fun.

A female slave at the Hotel du Nord came into the coffee-room one evening when I was there, and asked her master for some medicine. "You are not ill, and it is only an excuse to avoid work."—"Senhor," answered the negress, "there is One above who knows that I am very ill, and must have medicine; if you do not consent, I must die, and you will lose a good slave. I cost you above one hundred dollars, you will lose all." This was attacking the Frenchman on the right quarter, for she was placed under the care of a surgeon.

We were surprised one day by a visit from

the Frenchman we had landed at Paranagua; I understood him to say, that in consequence of the loss of the sloop he had been suspended from the service during the emperor's pleasure. This gentleman talked a good deal about *poudre*, he could do any thing with *poudre*—if he had but *poudre*, what he would not do!

Of a morning, at the Palace-square, I used to notice what provisions the gun-room stewards of the French men-of-war selected for the officers' mess. In a large basket was crammed ox-cheeks and pigs' heads, livers, sweetbreads, hearts, brains, tongues, and fish, and over these was spread a mighty *salade de toutes les espèces*, walled round by an inexhaustible quantity of *pain François*.

Towards the end of November, we again sailed from Rio Janeiro direct for Monte Video, Captain Stokes being anxious to join the Adventure without delay; and we had been about ten days at sea, when one afternoon a large ship appeared to the windward, under English colours, and fired three or four guns as a signal for us to bring-to. We made no doubt but that she was the Thetis man-of-war, bearing

> "Majestically near,
> Speed on her prow and terror in her tier,"

and we therefore fired a gun, hoisted our number, and began to slacken sail. When this ship came within a mile and a half of the Beagle she suddenly hauled down the English colours and hoisted Brazilian, and fired other guns, but Captain Stokes no sooner perceived the Brazilian flag than he appeared to be much vexed at having been detained, and gave immediate orders to clap on all sail, although the frigate was very anxious to speak us, and fired another gun, which we answered. She now gave us chase, but a breeze springing up we lost her in the night, and came to an anchor in Monte Video early the next day. Captain King had been here some time, and had purchased a small schooner, in order to facilitate the survey of the Straits of Magellan, (for to those inhospitable and tempestuous shores the ships were again about to proceed to pass the winter, either in Port Famine or Port Gallant,) and this vessel was to be commanded by one of the skilful officers from the Adventure.

As I had a few months previously made application to Captain Stokes for permission to secede from the expedition on the final departure of the Beagle, I accordingly, on the 21st of December, left the service, and luckily obtained a passage in the packet Rinaldo (Lieutenant Moore), then getting under weigh for Rio Janeiro, at which anchorage I left this vessel, the commander of her not being willing to take me to Falmouth under 50*l.* As no men-of-war were at that time homeward-bound, I most likely should have been placed in a very interesting situation (for people here are very fond of being paid) had I not fortunately met with Lieutenant Walkie, the commander of the Goldfinch packet, who most generously gave me a passage to England without the least hesitation.

THE END.

LONDON:
PRINTED BY W. WILCOCKSON, WHITEFRIARS.

Zeitfracht Medien GmbH
Ferdinand-Jühlke-Straße 7
99095 Erfurt, Deutschland
produktsicherheit@kolibri360.de